ISBN 978-0-265-17569-9
PIBN 10169856

BRIEF SKETCH.

OF THE

LIFE AND PUBLIC SERVICES

OF

JOHN SHERMAN

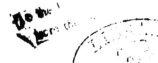

WITH SOME CONSIDERATIONS IN FAVOR OF HIS
NOMINATION IN 1888 AS THE

Republican Candidate for the Presidency.

BY

WILLIAM LAWRENCE.

PUBLISHED BY

THE SHERMAN LEAGUE,

OF CINCINNATI AND HAMILTON COUNTY.

1888

BRIEF SKETCH

OF THE

LIFE AND PUBLIC SERVICES

OF

JOHN SHERMAN

62

46L

WITH SOME CONSIDERATIONS IN FAVOR OF HIS
NOMINATION IN 1888 AS THE

REPUBLICAN CANDIDATE FOR THE PRESIDENCY.

BY

WILLIAM LAWRENCE.

PUBLISHED BY
THE SHERMAN LEAGUE,
OF CINCINNATI AND HAMILTON COUNTY.

1888

LIFE AND PUBLIC SERVICES

OF

JOHN SHERMAN.

SHERMAN AS A CANDIDATE FOR THE PRESIDENCY.*

When an eminent citizen, who through many years has rendered valuable services to the Republic and to humanity, is being prominently urged in all parts of the country for nomination as a candidate for the Presidency of the United States, it is natural that some interest should be felt, especially by young men, in his ancestry and early life. An accurate and able writer has given the following faithful sketch:

ANCESTRY AND EARLY LIFE OF JOHN SHERMAN.

JOHN SHERMAN's paternal ancestors emigrated from Essex County in Old England to Massachusetts and. Connecticut in New England at the time when those colonies rose suddenly, like the dragon's teeth sown by Cadmus, into full-grown strength — not, however, armed like those fabulous warriors with weapons for their own destruction, but with the virtues, the vigor, and the intelligence of the Anglo-Saxon race.

His grandfather, Taylor Sherman, of Norwalk, Connecticut, was an accomplished scholar and an able jurist, who received a seat on the Bench and who was a Commissioner of the Fire-lands Settlements, when

---

* This pamphlet is in part an enlargement of an article which appeared in the North American Review for November, 1887, in favor of Mr. Sherman's nomination as a candidate for the Presidency, and is in other respects a compilation.

in 1805 he went to Ohio to arrange some disputed boundary questions. While engaged in this service he became personally interested in tracts of land located in Sherman Township, Huron County; but he returned to Connecticut, where he died in 1815. He married early in life Elizabeth Stoddard, a lineal descendant of Anthony Stoddard, who emigrated from England to Boston in 1639. She was a sincere and honest woman, devoted to her husband and her children, and lived to a good old age, dying in Ohio about 1848. Charles Robert Sherman, their son (the father of John Sherman), was born and brought up at Norwalk, Connecticut, where he in due time commenced the study of the law in the office of his father, who was then associated with Judge Chapman. He was admitted to the Bar in 1810, and on the 10th of May of that year he married Mary Hoyt, also of Norwalk, who had grown up with him from childhood. She was a steadfast, true-hearted woman, devoted to her family and beloved by her friends. A few months after his marriage he went to Ohio in search of a home, leaving his wife in Connecticut. He arrived at Lancaster on his way to Cincinnati, and was so much pleased with the place and the people that he concluded to remain there. Receiving a cordial welcome, he was soon engrossed in the practice of his profession. The following season his wife came to him across the Alleghanies on horseback, carrying her infant child (afterward Judge Charles T. Sherman) on a pillow strapped before her saddle. It was a long and dreary road, beset with hardships, but Mrs. Sherman was fortunate in having as companions a considerable party of emigrants from her native region who sought on the western slope of the Alleghanies a new home.

Cheered by the presence of his wife and child, Charles Robert Sherman rapidly rose to eminence as an eloquent advocate, and as a judicious reliable counselor. His professional character was spotless, and while he would refuse clients when his conscience would not permit him to screen their wrong-doings, he was always ready to plead the cause of the innocent and oppressed without reward. While devoted to his profession, he extended his reading beyond his law-books, and was generally versed in the literature of the day. He was a prominent member of the Masonic fraternity, and filled the highest offices in the grand bodies of that order in Ohio.

During the pioneer years of Ohio, tradition records that its lawyers were obliged to travel over extensive circuits in practicing their profession. They were accustomed to accompanying the courts from county to county, and in this way to traverse a large extent of country. Those early days also commemorated the warmest personal friendships in the profession, as its members were forced into the most intimate companion-ship. They rode together on horseback, their saddle-bags stuffed with briefs, documents, law-books, clothing, and generally some creature delectation also. They were exposed in common to the same inclem-encies and impediments of travel; they lodged together at the same taverns, ate at the same tables, and slept in the same rooms, generally two in the same bed. Manly, jovial, and free-hearted, after a hard-fought day of professional antagonisms in court, they would crowd the evening hours with social amenities, winged with wit and merriment, with pathos, sentiment, and song.

In 1823 Mr. Charles R. Sherman was elected by the Legislature of Ohio to the Bench of the Supreme Court, and perhaps the only man in the State who doubted his ability for this high position was himself. He expressed fears that he lacked the ripe experience of years necessary to hear and determine cases of magnitude in a court of last resort; but he fully realized the large expectations of his professional friends and the public. His written opinions, published in Hammond's Reports of the Supreme Court of Ohio, demonstrated a mind of the choicest legal capabilities. They are clear, compact, comprehensive, and conclusive, and have since been respected by the Bar and the Courts in Ohio and other States as judicial opinions of the highest authority. Judge Sher-man won upon the Bench, as he had at the Bar, the affection and confi-dence of his professional associates. They esteemed him for his gentle and genial ways, for the brilliant flashes of his mind and the solid strength of his judgment, and above all for the stainless integrity of his character as a judge and as a man. The Supreme Court was then, under the pro-visions of the constitution, required to hold an annual term in each county of the State, two of the judges officiating. In every court-room in Ohio where Judge Sherman presided he made friends. His official robes were worn by him as the customary habiliments, and he was never haughty, austere, or overbearing on the Bench. He had thus entered upon the sixth year of his official term, in the full fruition of his matured intellect-ual powers and in the enjoyment of apparently robust physical health, when as he was about to hold a session of the Supreme Court at Lebanon he was suddenly and without any premonition stricken down with a fatal malady. The best medical aid was promptly summoned from Cincinnati, but in vain. A messenger hastened to Lancaster for Mrs. Sherman, but before she could reach Lebanon her husband had breathed his last. He died on the 24th of June, 1829, in the forty-first year of his age.

Mrs. Sherman was thus left a widow with eleven children. The oldest, Charles T. Sherman, eighteen years of age, was then at college, and the youngest was an infant about a month old. Her means were limited, her husband never having accumulated much property, and she had to depend upon what she had inherited from her father. Kind friends came to her assistance in her bereavement, and took charge of the oldest children. Mr. Thomas Ewing, a neighbor and friend of the deceased, adopted the third son, William Tecumseh, and procured his appointment as a cadet at West Point, where he was trained for his great services in upholding the Union and bearing its flag in triumph "from mountains to the sea."

John Sherman, the eighth child, was only six years of age when his father died and when the happy domestic circle was suddenly broken. His recollections are of the gradual scattering of the family until only four children remained with their mother, and in due time he also left. A cousin of his father, named John Sherman, a merchant at Mount Vernon, who was recently married, took the fatherless lad home with him in the spring of 1831, and he remained with him four years, attending school constantly, with the exception of occasional visits to his home. Many pleasant incidents of his life at Mount Vernon are remembered by the oldest citizens and by himself. The schools were very good, and his progress was rapid and satisfactory; but, according to the traditions, he was rather a wild and reckless boy, always in the lead in mischief and sport, of which some amusing anecdotes are told. At the age of twelve he returned to Lancaster with a view of going to Mr. Howe's Academy, then a rather famous school. He attended that institution constantly for two years, at the end of which time he was far enough advanced to have entered the sophomore class at college.

At that time, the spring of 1837, through the influence of Charles Sherman, he was tendered a position by Colonel Samuel R. Curtis (afterward a Representative in Congress) as junior rod-man on the Muskingum improvement, and gladly availed himself of the chance to make his own way in the world. He was then fourteen years old, tall and strong, more like a lad of sixteen or seventeen, and advanced in his studies, being well versed in most branches of mathematics, knowing a little Latin, and having studied the other branches necessary for his preparation for college. Two things stood in his way: First, the want of means; and second, his earnest desire to be independent and to relieve his friends of all care on his account. During his ride in a stage-coach from Lancaster to Zanesville, and thence to McConnellsville, he enjoyed the sense of freedom and independence, with all the hopes and anticipations of the future. At McConnellsville he met Colonel Curtis for the first time, was received very heartily, and at once made at home in his family and among his acquaintances. After a few days he was ordered to report to the Engineer Corps, then engaged in preparations for the Muskingum improvement. The long walk of sixteen miles which he took one summer's afternoon with James M. Love (now the United States District Judge of Iowa) was thought little of at the start, but was considered afterward as about the hardest day's work of his life, as up to that time he had never undertaken to walk so far. They arrived, fatigued and worn out, and joined the corps, then camping in tents where the day's work left them; but as the country around them was thickly populated the nights were usually spent in visiting the neighboring farmers, who were kind and hospitable. As Sherman and Love were new-comers they had not been invited out, when on the second night at their camp, as they were alone, a sudden storm came up, blew their tent down, drenched them with rain, and left them in a sorry plight for the rest of the night.

After the work was carried to maturity the corps was divided among the different stations where locks or canals were to be constructed. Sherman was stationed at Lowell as junior rod-man for Assistant Engineer Coffinbury. In the spring of 1838, by the resignation of the officer in charge of the work at Beverly, Sherman was temporarily placed in charge, and there remained during the rest of his service on the improvement. This necessarily devolved on him a considerable responsibility, including the measurement of excavations, embankments, and stone material, the necessary leveling for a lock to the canal, and a great variety of business growing out of the construction of a work that was to cost about $300,000. Mr. Sherman has always regarded the responsibility thus thrown upon him, and the necessary diligence and care in performing the duties assigned to him, as a better education than any he could possibly have had elsewhere in the same time. It taught him to study accuracy in details and close attention to business, and inspired self-confidence. In the severest months of winter work was necessarily suspended, especially in the construction of the dam and in laying the masonry of the lock. He was thus left a month or two of leisure in the winter of 1838-39 This he endeavored to occupy by a salt speculation, which was for a long time a subject of joke among his kindred and friends. He purchased a lot of salt and loaded it on a scow, intending to float with it and three or four men down the river to Cincinnati. The prospects of the speculation were very good, as salt was high at Cincinnati and low in Muskingum; but unluckily, within one day's float of the mouth of the river, Sherman's boat was frozen up tight, and remained there two months until the season passed by, and left him a loser instead of a gainer. He, however, when the river permitted, went to Cincinnati, where his brother Lampson P. Sherman lived as a member of the family of the somewhat famous Charles Hammond, then the editor of the Cincinnati Gazette. He there spent a week or two in the usual enjoyment of youths of his age, and had many long rambles about Cincinnati.

In the fall of 1838 the Whigs, who had been in power, were suddenly thrown out by the election, and during the following winter a new Board of Public Works commenced the common policy of making changes in the employes on the public works. Colonel Curtis, whose politics were well known, was removed from his position, in the spring of 1839, simply because he was a Whig. His subordinates were not changed for a time; but, as a sense of their gratitude to Colonel Curtis, most of them signed a letter expressing their confidence in him and their regret at the official separation. Some of these young men who signed this paper were Democrats and others were Whigs, but the letter was construed as an offense by Captain Wall, a member of the Board of Public Works in charge of the improvement, and all who had signed the letter were summarily turned out. So in the summer of 1839 young Sherman was removed from his humble position because he was a Whig.

Although but sixteen years of age, John Sherman was by birth and training an active, earnest Whig boy, and without much knowledge of the dispute between parties he was, without doubt, as honest in his opinions as many grown people who knew more of the subject-matter.

Upon being thus ousted he returned to Lancaster, and made up his mind to study law; but before doing so his earnest desire was to go to college and complete a regular course. During his service in the Engineer Corps he had improved himself by reading, by reviewing his studies, and by contact with men, so that he could readily enter the junior year, and that was his wish; but unfortunately no pecuniary means were available. Some of his kindred had been embarrassed by the revulsions of the panic of 1837, and most of them were too poor to aid him, and he was too proud to seek aid from others; so that, after a winter of rather listless study at Lancaster, upon the invitation of his brother Charles he determined to go to Mansfield to study law, keeping the hope of entering college in reserve.

Charles Sherman was then a good lawyer, in active practice, mostly as a commercial lawyer, unmarried, and nearly thirty years of age. John was just seventeen, tall, strong, and active. Mansfield was then a village of 1,100 inhabitants, in its earliest stage of growth, without pavements or other improvements, in the midst of a country which had been settled less than thirty years, but which was rapidly becoming peopled with good farmers, most of whom were of Pennsylvania descent and Democratic politics. It was known as the "Berks of Ohio," from its very large Democratic majorities. As a matter of course, any political ambition was entirely out of the question, and it was fortunate for the young man that it was so for many years. John Sherman's uncle, Jacob Parker, an old, well-educated lawyer, and a man of influence, lived in Mansfield, and took great interest in his nephew's progress. He constantly aided and directed him in his course of studies. After he had read Blackstone and Kent he was set at work on Coke upon Littleton, and kept three months at this driest of books, being frequently examined as to his progress. Judge Parker was a great lover of the Law of Tenures and of Ancient English Law. Soon afterward (while young Sherman was still a student) he became a Judge of the Common Pleas Court, and continued so until a short time before his death.

While studying law young Sherman regularly prepared the pleadings, and did a good amount of the office business of his brother, practiced before justices of the peace, prosecuted a great variety of business, and after the first year was entirely self-supporting, and lost all interest in his former desire to complete a collegiate course.

The Bar at Mansfield was then considered a very able one—as much so as any in Ohio. James Stewart, T. W. Bartley, and Jacob Brinkerhoff were then active practitioners, and all of them were subsequently judges of the higher courts; and a number of other lawyers of very respectable standing contested with them Quite a large number of law-students were then in Mansfield, among whom were Hon. Samuel J. Kirkwood (afterward Secretary of the Interior) and Hon. W. B. Allison (now United States Senator from Iowa), Frank Barker, and others, who were admitted to the Bar and attained distinction. These younger lawyers organized themselves into a moot court, which for a year or two was very useful, but finally broke up. The four years of life spent as a law-student, though longer than necessary, was still not without its value. Under the laws of Ohio young Sherman was compelled to wait until he was twenty-one years of age before he could be admitted, and impatiently did so, as he was prepared for admission before, and was restrained from engaging in practice before the court until the day of boyish emancipation came. Those who knew him then speak of him as having a quiet, determined manner, and, once started in a direction, he could not be turned aside until he had succeeded or satisfied himself beyond a doubt that he was not working to a successful result. He had no bad habits or evil companions, but gave his whole mind and attention to his professional studies. While not a jovial companion, in the usual acceptation of the term, he was always genial and affable to all, and seemed more desirous of winning friendship through respect than establishing a reputation for good-fellowship.

Mr. Sherman was admitted to the Bar on the 11th of May, 1844, at Springfield, Ohio, and he at once entered into partnership with his brother (Charles T.) at Mansfield. From that time forward he was constantly, actively, and profitably employed in the practice of his profession, until he was elected a member of Congress in 1854. Incessant in his application to business, conciliatory in his deportment, and identified with the people of Mansfield and the surrounding section, he soon occupied a high position in the courts. His oratorical powers were not of that old Roman school of declamation which was practiced by the Revolutionary fathers and their immediate descendants; but he argued his cases after a plain, blunt [logical], straight-forward [forcible] style, which secured him the attention of the court and won the confidence of the jury. His manner gave freshness and vigor to his legal arguments, as though his thoughts were spontaneous, and he was quietly drawing all the law and the facts from the case of his client. Occasionally, when deeply interested, he would speak with wonderful rapidity, and, although he was at times sarcastic, his words never carried a venomous sting. To work was apparently Mr. Sherman's ambition, and he succeeded. He not only studied with great care all cases in which he was retained, searching industriously for decisions bearing upon them, but he kept himself read up in the legal literature of the day. He also prosecuted his general reading, especially upon the *great public questions* of the period, and endeavored to ascertain the wishes of the people around him concerning them. No obstacle was ever permitted to remain in his way; and this, if we may believe Abraham Lincoln, is a family trait. When a revolt took place in the earlier part of the war for the suppression of the rebellion, and General William Tecumseh Sherman subdued it, one of the officers complained to President Lincoln that the General had been very severe in his language, and had said, if a similar disorder took place again, one of the old regiments should fire on the regiment of recruits that was so disorderly. The officer asked Lincoln whether he didn't think that severe. "Well," said Mr. Lincoln, "don't you trust those Shermans; they are so apt to do just as they say they will." The citizens of Mansfield found that their young lawyer when he undertook to do any thing was very apt to do it. . . . .

Shortly after Mr. Sherman was admitted to the Bar, his mother removed from her own home at Lancaster to Mansfield, where she and her two younger daughters kept house for him, and where she remained until her death in 1852, after her children were all married. In the winter of 1846–47 Mr. Sherman made his first visit to Washington, remaining nearly a mouth, during which time he became acquainted with most of the men of the day, and especially with Mr. Douglass, then a prominent Democratic leader, who treated him with great kindness, and who, but for his politics, would have won his hearty support. His recollections of this visit are quite vivid, and are carefully preserved in a series of interesting letters which he wrote to personal friends at home.

In the spring of 1848 Mr. Sherman was selected by the congressional district in which he lived as a delegate to the National Convention to be held at Philadelphia. When the convention was being organized, upon motion of Colonel Collyer, he was made a secretary of the body by the jocular remark that there was a young man there from the State of Ohio who lived in a district so strongly Democratic that he never could hope to get an office unless that convention gave him one, and with the laugh that this created Mr. Sherman advanced to his position. Mr. Defrees, of Indiana, afterward Public Printer, said there was a young man from Indiana in precisely the same situation, and moved that Schuyler Colfax be made assistant secretary. Colfax and Sherman walked up to the stand together. The position of the delegates at Philadelphia was one of high responsibility — each man had doubtless his sectional pride and personal feelings to influence him; but there was an overruling consideration. The enemy was in possession of the Capital — under whom could a change be effected? Who was there with pure integrity, tried patriotism, high abilities, and known principles who could rally the Whig forces and inspire them with confidence? The convention followed the example of the ancient Romans and sought an American Cincinnatus, whose disinterested virtues, simplicity of manners, and long public services had won for him a reputation which in the hour of peril filled the hearts of his countrymen, and sent them to seek him in his tranquil home to offer him the chief command of the Republic. The history of his life, as inscribed on the records of his country, was his recommendation; and they selected him because they knew him by his deeds, and felt positive that a civic wreath would be added to the victorious crown of him who "never surrendered.".

Mr. Sherman cordially supported the nomination and canvassed a portion of Ohio for him. "Old Zack" lost that State, but he was elected President and occupied the White House. During that same summer (on the 30th of August) Mr. Sherman was married to Miss Cecilia Stewart, the only child of Judge Stewart, of Mansfield, who came there from Western Pennsylvania. She is a lady of rare accomplishments, and capable of filling any social position, but domestic in her tastes, a thorough housewife, and kind to the poor and needy.

During the winter of 1848–49 the excitement about the discovery of gold in California became very strong. The first clear account received in Ohio was in a letter from Captain (now General) Sherman to his brother John, in which he stated clearly and at length the history of the discovery and its effect upon affairs in California. Mr. Sherman has this letter in his possession, and in view of subsequent events it is very interesting.

In the spring of 1849 Mr. Sherman built his house at Mansfield. It is a plain brick edifice, with a corner porch as seen from the front, and has since been remodeled by the addition of a mansard roof. This porch in summer is the Secretary's favorite resting-place, and up under the roof is his library and study. The house is surrounded by well-kept grounds, ornamented with a variety of shade-trees, through which a broad drive-way leads up to the entrance.

For years Mr. Sherman was very actively employed in the common country law practice of Ohio in those days. He rode the circuits of several counties, attended the courts, tried cases, collected debts, and besides transacted a variety of miscellaneous business. While he was a public-spirited and generous citizen, and far removed from any smallness in money-matters, he enjoyed the reputation of being a shrewd financier, who never made a mistake in his calculations concerning investments. It is stated by one who knew him well that he made it a rule, early in life, to lay aside at least $500 each year, and to regulate his expenditures in conformity with that determination. He never failed to do it; and when he saw this safely invested, then he used more—if there was more—for pleasure, or was more liberal in personal expenditures. About six years after he commenced the practice of law he embarked in the manufacture—then new to that part of Ohio—of flooring, doors, sashes, blinds, and other wood-work used in house-building. This investment was a profitable one, yielding him a handsome profit for a number of successive years.

In the Whig Convention of Ohio, held in 1850, Mr. Sherman took an active stand in favor of General Scott as the next Whig candidate for President, and made a speech which at that time was thought to have had great influence in directing public opinion in Ohio toward him. It was so well received that a proposition was made to nominate Mr. Sherman for Attorney-General; but the committee thought proper to renominate Henry Stanbury. It has been previously stated that John Sherman was a Whig boy; and as he grew older he became more wedded to the principles of Washington and Hamilton, John Marshall, Henry Clay, and Daniel Webster—principles that will live and illustrate the history of this country and of constitutional liberty through all coming time. The Whig party was eventually broken up by unscrupulous politicians; but its choicest principles were preserved and embedded into the creed of the Republican party. Those who had advocated them still assert with pride their title to the appellation of "an old Whig."

In the summer of 1852 Mr. Sherman was elected by the State Convention a senatorial delegate to the National Convention to be held at Baltimore. He attended that enthusiastic and able gathering, where he warmly supported General Scott, who was nominated. He advocated the selection of this old hero, not merely for his distinguished military services, but for his eminent qualities as a civilian, his honesty as a man, his integrity as a citizen, and his devotion to the Union, in defense of which he had poured out his life's blood, and for the perpetuation of which he had pledged "his life, his fortune, and his sacred honor." Returning to Ohio, Mr. Sherman participated in the canvass, but with very unsatisfactory results. While the election was pending he heard of the sudden death of his mother, and, relinquishing his remaining appointments, he returned home to Mansfield.

In the winter of 1853-54 Mr. Sherman opened a law-office in Cleveland, with the intention of removing there at some future time; but the proposition then pending to repeal the Missouri Compromise excited the greatest agitation and alarm throughout the State—greater than has been known at any period since. It shook all parties to their foundation. The bad policy of the movement, its want of faith, its threatened danger for the future, created a profound impression upon public opinion, and upon Mr. Sherman's own mind as well. Up to that time he had been what might be called a conservative Whig; anxious to avoid all discussions about slavery; feeling that it was wrong, indefensible, and ought to be abolished, but believing it was protected by the constitution, and therefore ought not to be assailed. This proposed repeal convinced him that the contest between freedom and slavery must come, that it was unavoidable, and that the proper and true way was to enter the lists. First, upon the ground that in no event should slavery derive any benefit from the repeal of the Missouri Compromise; and, second, that it should as rapidly as possible be abolished in all the Territories of the United States. When the Congressional Anti-Nebraska Convention, as it was called, met, composed of those who had been members of the Democratic, the Whig, and the Freesoil parties, great difficulty existed in forming a fusion of opposing elements, jealous of each other. The choice finally fell upon Mr. Sherman, who was then but thirty-one years of age; and while a prominent Whig, was not so prominent as to be subject to bitter hostility from opposing factions. There was a good deal of feeling in the northern counties of the district because he was not up to their standard of opinion on the slavery question; but his personal canvass through the district tended to dissipate these fears, and he was elected, receiving 8,617 votes against 5,794 votes for Wm. D. Lindsley, who then represented the district in Congress.

Mr. Sherman attended and was president of the first Ohio Republican State Convention, in 1855, which nominated Salmon P. Chase for Governor, and participated in the organization of the great Republican party, which was at once progressive, yet prudent; radical, yet conservative; neither afraid of the new because it was new, nor contemptuous of the old because it was old. His acuteness of intellect, indefatigable industry and wisdom, which is master of his temper, gave him a commanding position in the ranks of the new political movement, and since that time his life has been a part of the public life of the country.

Mr. Sherman took his seat in the House of Representatives of the Thirty-fourth Congress on the third of December, 1855, six years before the war — six years of political strife, of civil commotion, ripening into open rebellion, which formed an eventful career in our political history. Those who were meditating the establishment of a new empire, based upon the enslavement of the African race, were menacing, bitter, and uncompromising; while affiliated with them by party ties, though not in sympathy, were Cass, Douglass, and other northern Democrats, who vainly struggled against the current of events. Among the great questions debated during these six years were the repeal of the Missouri Compromise, the Dred-Scott Decision, the Imposition of Slavery upon Kansas, the Fugitive-slave Law, the national expenditures and receipts, grave questions of finance, and other kindred measures involving the very existence of the Republic.

Mr. Sherman brought with him into the halls of the National House of Representatives, at the commencement of the discussion of these vital questions, the habits of business and of patient labor and of thorough investigation which his early training had given him; and he very soon acquired the respect of all his associates and the confidence of his political friends in no ordinary degree. He often participated in debate, and by his full comprehension of the subject, the result of careful and dispassionate examination, and by his familiar acquaintance with public affairs, rose rapidly in reputation. A good speaker, a clear thinker, and a logical reasoner, his strong point was in the proportion of his faculties to each other, which made him, without being an extraordinary man in any one particular, equal to the greatest occasion and to every difficulty. In times of unexampled excitement and difficulties he conducted himself with such dign ty that he impressed all who approached him with profound respect, and yet inspired all with affection, esteem, and confidence; and to this end he united a firm fidelity to his principles, his party, and friends, which was proof against all changes and disasters, combining the *fortiter in re.* with the *suaviter in modo.* His bitterest political foes were disarmed by his calm and philosophical bearing, and his best friends shrank from all attempts to sway him from the path of duty, from his honest convictions, and from his loyalty to the Union.*

The subsequent career of Mr. Sherman is well known to the country. Some of his public acts and utterances are presented in the following pages.

SHERMAN AS A CANDIDATE FOR THE PRESIDENCY—HIS PUBLIC SERVICES, ABILITY, AND AVAILABILITY.

At Toledo, on the 28th of July, 1887, the Ohio Republican Convention, composed of 723 delegates, representing every part of the State, *unanimously* adopted a resolution declaring that "the Republicans of Ohio . . have just pride in the record and career of John Sherman as a member of the Republican party, and as a statesman of fidelity, large experience, and great ability." And it declares that the Republicans of Ohio "respectfully present his name to the people of the

---

*The foregoing sketch is taken from "The Life and Public Services of John Sherman," written in 1880 by Ben: Perley Poore, the veteran and able journalist, who, up to that time perhaps had better and more extended opportunities for giving a correct estimate of the statesmen of the country than any one of the great body of intelligent and useful men of his honorable profession in the whole country.

United States as a candidate, and announce our hearty and cordial support of him for that office."

This resolution merely *emphasized a demand* in unmistakable terms from every State in the Union, a year in advance of the national nominating convention, that Mr. Sherman shall be the candidate.

The Republicans of Ohio, *unanimously* voicing their own wishes, do not present Mr. Sherman as a candidate for the inadequate reason that he was "born" in the State, or that his residence here has made him "a favorite son," but on the *solid ground*, stated in the resolution, that "his career as a statesman began with the birth of the Republican party; he has grown and developed with the growth of that organization; his genius and patriotism are stamped upon the records of the party and the statutes and constitution of the country, and believing that his nomination for the office of President would be wise and judicious."

SHERMAN UNANIMOUSLY INDORSED IN OHIO AS A CANDIDATE.

This resolution was not adopted on the mere motion of a member of the convention, but was reported by the Committee on Resolutions as *a part of the State platform*, and thus made an *issue in the campaign*, on which a Governor, Lieutenant-Governor, Judges of the Supreme Court, and other State officers were to be voted for, and as a means of *giving strength* to the ticket. Prior to the convention the inquiry had occasionally been made whether it was *expedient* to make such a question in the canvass, but when the convention met the Committee on Platform unanimously agreed to the resolution, which was, as already stated, adopted without one dissenting vote in the convention. During the campaign, Governor Foraker, a candidate for re-election, in referring to this subject in a public speech, said :

"John Sherman has been put upon a *sure train*, with a *free pass* in his own name, and I do not know of *any one* [Republican] from the river to the lake who wishes to take it from him. [Loud applause.] John Sherman has *no* such train-wreckers to avoid as Allen G. Thurman can give an account of."*

---

*Speech at Caldwell, Ohio, September 10, 1887.

SHERMAN'S POPULARITY IN OHIO.

The result demonstrated alike the wisdom of inserting in the platform the plank above mentioned and of thus making the *direct issue* for Sherman. It demonstrated his *great popularity*, as well as that of the candidates nominated and the *cause* they all represented. The Republicans elected their entire State ticket; the majority of the Republican candidate for Governor over his opponent being 5,868 votes *greater* than two years previous, and 11,538 greater than the similar majority on Secretary of State in 1886, and the Republicans carried the election in nearly every close or doubtful district for Senators and Representatives in the General Assembly.

This the *latest evidence* of Mr. Sherman's *popular strength* is merely supplementary to other and preceding proofs on this subject. His popularity has stood the test *without one failure*. Though never a Democrat, he was *four times* elected a Representative in Congress by *solid majorities*, in a district always *previously strongly Democratic*.

The result of Ohio elections has always been uncertain; even during the war, in 1862, the Democrats elected a majority of Representatives in Congress. In all of the *five legislative elections* with Mr. Sherman as a prospective candidate for Senator, and when his merits and popular strength were put to the test, the Republican party carried the State, and he was elected. In other years Ohio went Democratic, and elected Thurman, Pendleton, and Payne as Senators. In 1883 many leading Republicans of Ohio insisted that Mr. Sherman should, as *the most available citizen*, leave his place in the Senate, to lead the Republican party to victory as a candidate for Governor; but other counsels prevailed, and Hoadly, the Democratic candidate, was elected.

With these almost unexampled evidences of Mr. Sherman's commanding strength for popular favor in Ohio, the question is no longer an open one as to the choice of the voters of this State or of his availability. And this conclusion can not be changed, or his nomination as a candidate for the Presidency in 1888 be rendered the less desirable or expedient, even if in some one or more of the congressional districts of the State a delegation should be found preferring some other candidate. A solid, united delegation in a State with four million of people, and with each congressional district acting for itself, would be almost unprecedented.

The real question for the National Nominating Convention to determine, so far as it is to be governed by considerations of past and prospective popular successes of the candidate, is whether *he has proved* that he has real and deserved popular favor, confidence, and strength.

Ohio has resolved this question *beyond all controversy in favor of Mr. Sherman.* And the effect of this upon the nomination in 1888 can not be doubted. *Ohio has never failed in securing the nomination and election of any of her citizens* upon whom she "heartily and cordially united," as she did upon Harrison, Hayes, and Garfield, and now does on Sherman.

This *continuous, unbroken, unfaltering,* and cordial popular support of Mr. Sherman has no parallel in the person of any other citizen of Ohio in her whole history. It rests on his unquestioned ability, his integrity, his great and meritorious public services; but it has been all the more earnest, zealous, and enthusiastic because in his intercourse with his fellow-men he has been invariably genial in his manners, courteous to all without regard to creed, color, or condition, and affable in the broadest and most generous sense of that term.* The humblest citizen has always felt that he could approach Mr. Sherman with freedom and feel at ease in his presence, because he would be met with kindly treatment and generous sympathy.

In the great duties and responsibilities of high office, in the perilous times of the Republic, he met unjust or unreasonable demands with firm and relentless resistance, and neither extended favors nor gave sympathy to those who made them.

In the pressing duties imposed upon him by the high public trusts he has occupied, he never sacrificed public interests for private favor or to secure personal friendships. To those who preferred he should have done otherwise he has neither been genial nor of ready access. But there is no man in public life more approachable, courteous, and genial than is John Sherman. This will be fully attested by all who really know him, and the popular favor which he has so long, so uniformly and firmly maintained in Ohio is itself unanswerable evidence on this subject.

The same elements of his public and private life which have made him

---

* The well-known able, though strongly Democratic, correspondent of the Cincinnati Enquirer ("Taylor") reports in that paper an interview with Mr. Sherman June 15, 1887, and prefaces it by saying:

"It is quite the thing to talk of Senator Sherman as cold and adamantine in his intercourse with his fellow-men, but for the life of me I can't understand how that idea became so widespread and general. There is a certain dignity about the distinguished statesman that well befits a man of his great public career, but there is no brusque statuesqueness about it, such as characterizes little men who reach lofty positions, and must needs stand as rigid as graven images, lest they topple over and make an exhibition of themselves in the dust. The Senator is quite as suave and fully as companionable as his brother, the General, and I have never failed to find him a most entertaining gentleman upon the whole range of topics, and reprehensible only in the miserable politics to which he clings."

The same opinion is expressed by another Democratic correspondent, quoted under the "Financial" portion of this pamphlet.

available in securing and maintaining political power in Ohio, have made
and will make him so in all the States as a candidate for the Presidency
in 1888.

THE REQUISITE QUALIFICATIONS FOR THE PRESIDENCY — SHERMAN HAS THEM ALL.

Among all the eminent men named as "possible Presidents,"* it may
be said, without disparagement to any, that some one, by reason of long
service, of experience, and for other reasons, may for the next election
be a more desirable candidate than any other.

Availability, resting on solid merits and services, including such as
fit a man to be President, should determine the choice.

We must distinguish between popular demonstrations of *friends* and
true popularity, which is not embarrassed by powerful, numerous, and
implacable enemies.   Mr. Sherman enjoys THIS *true popularity* more than
any candidate prominently mentioned.

A President is required to originate and recommend measures for the
consideration of Congress.†   A statesman with *large opportunities*, who
never originated or *carried into execution* any great measure, does *not* present all the qualities desirable in a President.   Mr. Sherman has "demonstrated his faith by his works."

Among the desirable qualities in a presidential candidate are these:
He should have *great learning*, *practical ability*, and *experience*, especially in
the line of statesmanship; he should comprehend the *rights*, the *industrial*
and *other interests* of the people, and the relation of these rights and
interests to each other; he should maintain principles of public policy
which will secure and promote them all in just harmony; for the conditions which now exist in the country, he should be an *able lawyer;* he
should have "the courage of his convictions;" the evidence of these
should be found in *public measures* perfected of record, and in *public
policies* carried into *practical execution*, not in barren promises or declamation; he should have the requisite recognized moral qualities, including
the character and *reputation for integrity*, which can not be justly assailed,
and he should have, and with the qualities named and as a sequence
thereof generally will have, *availability*.

Mr. Sherman fills the full measure of all these qualities and qualifica-

---

* The substance of a portion of the pages which follow was published in the New York
North American Review for November, 1887.

† Constitution, Art. II., Sec. 3.

tions, and *much more*, and, tried by these tests, he is the leading candidate of the Republican party; and, in the ability to harmonize and unite all interests and secure support, he is the most popular candidate of any party.

SHERMAN'S CLAIMS TO THE PRESIDENCY.

It is sometimes said that no man can have any "claims" to office. This is to say, "Republics are ungrateful." It is not true. He who has devoted *his life* to the public service, and has rendered *more* and *more valuable* public service than any other, and retains in full vigor of body and mind—*mens sana in corpore sano*—all the great qualities to make him-self *as useful*, if not more so, as any other can as yet be, has *claims* of the highest order to public favor. He who has been thus "faithful over *many* things" should be made ruler over a great nation.

SOME OF THE GROUNDS ON WHICH SHERMAN'S AVAILABILITY RESTS.

Political sagacity points to *Sherman as a candidate who will avoid antagonisms*, and have in more than a *united party* that *popularity born of great qualities and great achievements* He has the availability which results from great ability, long experience, practical conservative statesmanship, an intimate knowledge of all the interests of the country, a thorough acquaintance with the people and resources of every State, with the workings of our dual system of government in all departments, and in their relations to each other and to foreign nations. He is available because he has the highest order of executive ability, is efficient and profound in all that fits a man to be President, and has a record unblemished, and integrity unassailed and unassailable.

Mr. Sherman is now urged as a candidate for the Presidency, not by disparaging other eminent and good men, but because his greater services give him stronger claims and better fit him for the great office; he can unite and solidify the Republican forces; he can attract outside support; and so is the leading and most popular candidate mentioned.

It is not possible to give all the reasons which prove this, but it will be shown that, with TWELVE DIFFERENT CLASSES, comprising ALL, he is an available candidate, and with most of them he is the most available. His *opinions* are not left to conjecture. "He is the only man in the United States Government whose views on all questions of public affairs

in extenso are obtainable in book form " or otherwise.* His public services—what he *has done*—is as fully a matter of public record as his
opinions. With *him* as a candidate, the people would take no risks—
they would make no doubtful experiment.

A presentation of the claims of Mr. Sherman, and of *all* the reasons
which make his nomination more desirable, "judicious, and wise" as the
candidate of 1888 than that of any other citizen, would comprise in some
measure his biography and in full measure the history of his public
services, which would largely comprehend the history of the Republic
since he entered Congress, on the 4th of March, 1855, and a contrast
with the history of other great nations and the previous history of our
own. This is not now practicable.

But *some* of the reasons are so apparent as to challenge universal attention and assent. They will now be presented, recognizing *availability*
as a merited result of services rendered, qualities possessed, and opinions
entertained , by Mr. Sherman, which have drawn and will draw to his
support in harmonious relations all the great interests of the country, so
that his labors may bless the land in the future as in the past.

I.

THE LABORING MEN — THE LABOR PARTY.

I. MR. SHERMAN *is the leading and most popular Republican candidate in
this, that he can command more of the votes of the laboring men than
any other.*

It is not assumed that others with *equal opportunities might not* have
secured equal claims in this respect ; but the fact remains that *now* he
is justly to be regarded as, *par. excellence,* THE candidate having claims
beyond others. The toilers of the country, engaged in mechanical
industry, in factories, workshops, mines, forests, and labor in various
forms, have recently effected *organizations,* some *industrial,* others with a
view to secure the just rewards of their labor, and otherwise to promote

---

* Bronson's Life, 54: Sherman's Speeches, one volume, New York, 1879.

their interests by separate political party action. A presidential candidate, in other respects acceptable, who can *save the Republican party from disintegration* by their vote, will be elected. They will be an important factor in the next contest. Mr. Sherman is *the* candidate who can satisfy their just demands. Like all intelligent American citizens, most of these voters can be made to see that their *rights* and *interests* must be intrusted to *one* of the *two* great political parties, and that Mr. Sherman is in sympathy with all their just demands. Among their wants are these: *employment*, just *compensation* for services, payment therefor in *good money*, and a public policy which will in other respects secure their welfare. No man in Congress has done more, and no candidate for the Presidency so much as Mr. Sherman to secure the enactment of protective tariff laws, the chief object of which is to give employment to labor, and by making a demand therefor to insure it a just reward. The object of such tariff is "to secure to American citizens the privilege of supplying *every article* which can be produced as well in the United States as in other countries, and sufficiently to supply American wants. Such a tariff makes a *demand* for and *gives employment* to the labor of American citizens, and thereby aids in securing *just compensation*."* *One half* of all our manufacturing industries are dependent on a protective tariff for their continued existence.

Mr. Sherman, in his Nashville speech, March 24, 1887, shows that *one half of all manufactured articles are protected* by the tariff laws. He says:

"The domestic production of manufactured articles in the United States for the year 1886 is roundly estimated at $5,500,000,000, *of which amount about one half*, or say $2,500,000,000, *are domestic articles which compete with foreign productions*. The amount of the importations from abroad in 1886 was of the value of $625,000,000. The revenue received from the duties on these articles amounted to $188,000,000, making an average rate of duty of about 30 per cent. The general idea of the Democratic party is to levy these duties by such a rate approaching an *ad valorem* average rate as probably would produce the requisite revenue. The Republican idea is practically embodied in the tariff laws as they now exist. . . . Of the $625,000,000 of goods imported,

---

* Ohio Republican platform, July 28, 1887.

A citizen (Robert J. Williams), prominent among those engaged in labor movements, says: "American [Democratic] free trade means that vast foreign importations would be very encouraging to *foreign labor*; that domestic wages shall not exceed foreign wages; that American labor shall be compelled to compete with the world of [cheap] labor." And he demands that "importations [of articles] that can be raised or made in the United States . . must be shut out with customs tariff, in order that *American labor may have less competition.*"

$211,000,000, or more than one third, are now admitted duty free. The remaining $414,000,000 are subject to duties varying from 10 per cent to over 100 per cent. It is the general policy of the law to admit free of duty all articles of foreign production that can not be produced in this country, for which we have not the natural soil or climate, and yet which are in common use in every family here, such as tea, coffee, and similar articles."

Mr. Sherman is *pre-eminently* the advocate of *good money.* He, more than any other, is *the author* of our present currency system, and, as will be hereafter indicated, *has done more,* in the Senate and as Secretary of the Treasury, to secure the payment of honest labor in *honest money* than any other living statesman. As President he can be relied on to earnestly recommend to Congress wise legislation in the interest of labor, and to *faithfully carry into execution* all legislation on the subject. His public *utterances and acts even before the existence of any political or other organization in the interest of laboring men* prove this. He voted for the act of Congress of July 1, 1862, in aid of agricultural and mechanical colleges ; the *eight-hour law* of June 28, 1868; the act of May 18, 1872, to prevent its evasion; the act of June 27, 1884, to create the Bureau of Labor; and the joint resolution of August 21, 1886, as to *prison labor.*

After his last re-election to the Senate, a reception was tendered to him and held at Columbus, Ohio, January 14, 1886, when, in addressing the members of the Senate and House of Representatives, he, among other matters, said :

"As *labor* is the *foundation of all production,* of all prosperity, and is performed by the great body of our people, *every measure* should have for *its chief object the protection of labor* and *of those who labor,* and to *secure for them the largest possible share in the comforts of life.* Above all there should be some prompt and efficient remedy, by arbitration or summary process, to settle the disputes that often arise between laborers and operators as to rate of wages, hours of work, and the like, and this remedy should be a condition of every act of incorporation granted by the State.

"Every opportunity for education, improvement, and advancement should be afforded to all classes alike, without distinction of race, color, nativity, or creed. Good government depends upon the equal voice and vote of all, and this can only be secured by the diffusion of intelligence, and fair and just treatment of all branches of industry.

"The protection of property is the cause of the great body of the expenses of a government, and therefore acquired property should pay the great body of the taxes imposed by law. In this respect the laws of Ohio have always been just and fair, though sometimes oppressive, especially to the farmers, whose capital, easily ascertained, is sometimes made to bear an unequal share of the burdens of taxation. I have often thought that many modes could be devised of indirect taxation on the sale of articles which are not a prime necessity, and on special employments and corporations created by law, that would equalize taxation and reduce the rate."

In a public address at Cincinnati, March 26, 1887, Mr. Sherman said: *

"I have traversed more than once every State and Territory of the United States. . . There is a party organized in this country, with whose aims and purposes I have the most profound sympathy, calling itself the Workingmen's party. . . . I desire for myself (and as a Republican I speak for the Republican party), and my party desires to the very utmost, in every legal and proper way, to advance the interests of the workingmen of America, because they are the foundation on which our great superstructure is built. . . . The first effect of these separate organizations, by whatever name they may be called, is to weaken that party [Republican] which, according to the judgment of the men who join it [separate organization], on the whole has very generally proved satisfactory."

Again, in speaking of the laboring men, he said to them:

"You have a right to get together to hold your meetings, to discuss your interests, to argue with each other, to get as much wages for your labor as you can by co-operation. Indeed I think co-operation is one of the great safeguards. I believe the time is not far distant when the mechanic will get some portion of the surplus earnings by co-operation. His labor is a part of the capital, and, if it could be so arranged, for a division of the results of the labor co-operation is the best form by which it could be done."

Again he spoke of the laboring man, "whose reasonable demands ought always to be heard and always to be heeded."†

And in the same speech he emphatically indorsed the Ohio Republican platform of 1887, declaring adherence to the public policy which

---

* In the same speech he shows that a Republican Legislature in Ohio passed the eight-hour law, the bill for the payment in money of wages every fifteen days, the anti-Pinkerton law, etc. And see his speech at Portsmouth, Ohio, September 28, 1886; discussion in Senate February 23, 1887, Congressional Record, Vol. XVIII, page 2376.

The "National View," of Washington City, one of the newspaper organs of the labor interest, of which Lee Crandall is manager, in its issue of April 23, 1887, published the Cincinnati speech in full; and in the same number appears an article by a prominent labor advocate, who says:

"When John Sherman speaks out as he did at Cincinnati, and recognizes the laborer as having rights that demand protection, and conceding the justice of his claims for higher consideration and more positive legislation, I am encouraged to hope for the 'good time coming,' when all labor shall have a just reward and an equal chance in the race for life. . The fact that he [Sherman] reaches out a helping hand is so much to his credit, and shows that *he is on the right track.* The speech . . needs only to be read to impress the mind with the cogency of the reasoning and the spirit of real progress which animates every line. The conviction of its *honesty* and *earnestness* is so apparent, one can not help but respect and admire."

† Speech at Toledo, Ohio Republican State Convention, July 28, 1887.

welcomes "to our shores the well-disposed and industrious immigrant, who contributes by his energy and intelligence to the cause of free government," yet urging Congress "to pass such laws . . as shall protect us from the inroad of the anarchist, the communist, the polygamist, the fugitive from justice, the insane, the dependent paupers, the vicious and criminal classes, contract labor in every form, under any name or guise; and all others who seek our shores not to become a part of our civilization and citizenship, who acknowledge no allegiance to our laws, no sympathy with our aims and institutions, but who come among us to make war upon society to *diminish the dignity and rewards of American workingmen and degrade our labor to their level.*" *

---

*Many other speeches might be quoted; but as it is not practicable to give all, it is deemed appropriate here to give extracts from only two others.

Mr. Sherman in his Wilmington (Ohio) speech, September 15, 1887, said:

"If there is any just and practical measure of public policy that will tend to advance the interests of labor or laboring men, the Republican party is now and has been ready and willing to adopt it. Every measure in their interest in the statutes of Ohio and of the United States has been put there by the Republican party. The homestead law, the eight-hour law, the contract emigrant law, and that great system of public policy to protect their labor from undue competition by protective duties on imported goods, have been the work of the Republican party. The statute books of Ohio are full of laws to protect their homes and household effects, to guard them in the mines and workshops, to secure their wages by lien and preference laws, to restrain the employment of infants and women. The last Republican Legislature passed many laws for their benefit. I ask them to point out when and where the Republican party has failed to do justice to the laboring men. Our long struggle for thirty years has been to secure every man's liberty and equal rights. It is only when Socialists seek to strike down all the rules of social order which dignify the homes of poor and rich alike, or when Communists seek to enjoy the property acquired by the honest labor of others, or when Anarchists seek to tear down all the institutions of modern civilization, that the Republican party, as the conservative party of the country, resists their demands. These men are criminals and not laborers. They dishonor the word laborer, who only seeks the free and full enjoyment of the fruits of his labor, and will neither rob nor steal his neighbor's property."

In his Springfield (Ohio) speech, October 12, 1887, Mr. Sherman said:

"Laboring men also have the free right of organization by trades unions or any other form by which they may lawfully influence and control the rate of wages and hours of employment and all the conditions of their contract. This right of organization is as clear and complete to them as it is to the capitalists who combine their money into a corporation, or the many corporations that combine to control the market. Both laboring men and capitalists can organize to improve their condition. The only limit imposed upon both, for it applies to both, is that no unlawful violence or terror shall be used, and that criminal acts shall be avoided. It is the common interest of both parties that lock-outs and strikes should never be resorted to except under extreme circumstances, and I am glad to see that upon this subject many of the enlightened leaders of the workingmen, especially Mr. Powderly, give wise advice. [Applause.] My own observation has been that the great body of the strikes have resulted to the injury of laboring men, while lock-outs by capitalists have often been the cause of their ruin. Moderation and good sense and good humor between persons whose interests are often the best way to an honorable settlement of what appeared to be an unavoidable contest.

"Now, as to these controversies that occur between laboring men and capitalists, the Republican party has shown, both in the State and the Nation, its willingness to pass all reasonable laws desired by laboring men. I could enumerate these laws by the score; and, besides that, I can assure you that whenever any measure devised by you is presented to the Republicans in Congress or the State Legislature, you will find them willing and ready to listen and to adopt any thing that seems consistent with the public safety, with a hearty desire to carry out your wishes and to promote your interests.

"There are three classes who call themselves laborers, but in nearly every case are shirks or cranks, calling themselves Anarchists, Socialists, or Communists. These I regard as *quasi* criminals, as enemies of mankind, and, more than all, as enemies of the honest laborer who seeks to improve his condition, and hopes by honest industry and economy to attain for himself and his family a home, and property and independence. There is no excuse for Anarchists in this country. This is a Government of the people. They were organized to resist

SHERMAN FAVORS THE EXCLUSION OF CHINESE LABOR.

As a part of the same policy of protecting American workingmen, Mr. Sherman *is earnestly in favor of the exclusion of Chinese labor from our shores.*

Prior to the treaty proclaimed April 14, 1846, between the United States and China, the latter country admitted no commerce from ours. This treaty, to a certain extent, opened *five* ports of China to American trade; but American missionaries to the Celestial Empire were then unknown.

The treaty of January 26, 1860, provided that those American citizens "who *quietly* profess and teach" the principles of the Christian religion and "Chinese converts shall not be harassed or persecuted on account of their faith."

The "Burlingame" treaty of February 5, 1870, provided that "citizens of the United States in China *of every religious persuasion* . . and Chinese converts shall enjoy *entire liberty of conscience, and be exempt from all disabilities* or *persecution* on account of their religious faith or worship." Provisions were made in these treaties for commercial intercourse.

Thus the *way was open for American commerce, for American citizens to reside and trade in China, and for American missionaries* to prosecute there the work of evangelization. These were great achievements.

It was not then foreseen that Chinese laborers might flock into our country in *such numbers* and of *such character* as to seriously undermine the interests of American laborers.

When this fact became apparent it required *the highest type of states-*

---

tyranny, and when they propose to murder emperors and kings and privileged nobility they have at least the ground-work of oppression and wrong. In this country there are no privileged classes. Our history shows that the poorest lads of the day may rise to the dignity of the highest office in the Republic. And so with the Socialists, they aim to strike at the laws of society, of husband and wife, parent and child, guardian and ward, to break up the family home and all the social habits that are endeared to our people. If they want to practice Socialism, let them go to Kamschatka, to the Equator, or to Utah, where exceptional conditions exist. And so with the Communist, the man who wants to divide up with the honest, provident, and thrifty workingman, who wants to rob the rich man of his capital, will want another divide after two or three weeks' trial. We have no room in this country for this hell-brood of uneasy idlers, unwilling to work, but willing to enjoy the fruits of other men's labors. [Cheers.]

"I desire, in this connection, to express my hearty concurrence in the admirable letter of Cardinal Gibbons to Mr. Powderly, published in yesterday's papers. Coming from so eminent authority of a Christian Church, it is entitled to the highest consideration and respect and states clearly and impressively the distinction between the Knights of Labor and kindred associations, who wish only to improve their condition by careful and honest means, and the criminal schemes of Anarchists, Communists, and Socialists to break down the laws by which society is organized, and the social ties and rights of property upon which the fabric of civilization rests."

manship to save our commerce with China and Japan, to protect American citizens engaged in trade in those countries, and save American missionaries in the enjoyment of their privileges from *persecution* and from expulsion. In this condition of affairs the subject of excluding Chinese laborers from our shores was broached and discussed among our people and in Congress during the administration of President Hayes.

Many eminent statesmen *who favored the exclusion of Chinese laborers* believed that any *efficient legislation* by Congress for that purpose would *violate our treaty relations* with China, would *seriously impair our commerce* with that country, and endanger the safety of American citizens there residing and missionaries there prosecuting their labors. The "Burlingame" treaty "recognized the right of the citizens of either country to visit or *reside·in* the other."* Thus Congress was confronted with the *difficulty* and *danger* of excluding Chinese laborers, to do which would violate treaty stipulations, bring national dishonor, and imperil the rights and safety of our own citizens.

Accordingly President Hayes opened up negotiations with China, with a view to secure the exclusion, but at the same time imperil no one of our rights or interests. In this he was *cordially* and *efficiently* aided by Mr. Sherman, then Secretary of the Treasury.

These negotiations finally resulted in two treaties under President Arthur's administration, both proclaimed October 5, 1881 (22 U. S. Stat. 826–828); one regulating and saving American commerce, the other authorizing the exclusion of Chinese laborers from the United States, without imperiling any right of American citizens secured by previous treaties.

Our commercial and other rights and interests having thus been secured, and the way opened up for efficient legislation for the exclusion of Chinese laborers—a policy which Mr. Sherman *always* favored—he voted in the Senate for the bill, which became the act of Congress of July 5, 1884, to secure this object.†

---

* Vol. II., Blaine's Twenty Years of Congress, p. 651.

† See Blaine's Twenty Years of Congress, Vol. II., p. 651; 13 Cong. Record, 1747, 1749, 1751, 2551, 2606, 2610, 2615; Act of Congress May 6, 1882, 22 U. S. Stat. 58; see Cong. Record, Vol. XV., p. 5938. He said in the Senate, May 9, 1882, Cong. Record, Vol. XIII., p. 1748:

"When this debate commenced I had no more doubt about the necessity and propriety of voting for a bill on this subject than I had as to any ordinary act of legislation, because I had become convinced that, although it was exceptional legislation, contrary to the general habits of our country, yet the dangers that threatened our Pacific coast and might extend further and further eastward, did demand that we should pass some law to restrain and limit this immigration: but it does seem to me, on consideration, that in the very first act that is proposed under the treaty we have gone not only to the extreme of the treaty, but we have gone beyond the reasonable bounds of the treaty."

On April 5, 1882 (Congressional Record, Vol. XIII., page 2610), he said: "There is but little dispute that some provision of law should be made to restrain the importation of the

This act (23 U. S. Stat. 115) was designed to execute and carry into effect the treaty stipulations, giving a right to exclude Chinese laborers. It specified a time within which " the coming of Chinese laborers to the United States " is suspended, and then provides that " it shall not be lawful for any Chinese laborer to come from any foreign port or place, or having so come, to remain within the United States." It then makes provision for carrying the act into effect, prescribes penalties, etc.

Thus the whole subject has been so far disposed of in a manner to preserve national honor, to sacrifice no right of American citizens, to secure the privileges of American missionaries, and yet secure the object in view.

In the delicate and difficult work of securing these results, requiring the highest skill of diplomacy and statesmanship, Mr. Sherman shares with others the honors of the achievements. He has supplemented his labors by efforts more perfectly to secure the exclusion.

On the 29th of April, 1886, as Chairman of the Committee on Foreign Relations, he reported back to the Senate a bill amendatory of the Chinese acts, and May 26, 1886, he made a speech on the bill favoring the restriction.* Thus his record on all questions affecting labor and laborers must be eminently satisfactory. Nor is this all.

SHERMAN'S SYMPATHIES WITH LABORING MEN—THE EXECUTION OF THE LAWS IN THEIR FAVOR.

One important consideration is too often overlooked. The most useful laws, when intrusted to their enemies for execution, are *so* executed, or *not* executed, as practically to defeat their purpose. The *sympathies* and *opinions* of executive officers have much to do with the

---

class of Chinese laborers into this country which has been flowing into it for the last fifteen or twenty years."

On April 22, 1886, he reported back from the Committee on Foreign Relations a bill supplementary and amendatory to the above act (Cong. Record, Vol. XVII., p. 3957). As chairman of the committee he had charge of this bill and pressed it to a vote in the Senate, where it passed June 1, 1886. (Cong. Record, Vol. XVII., p. 5110.) During the debate on this bill, on May 26, 1886, he said (Cong. Record, Vol. XVII., p. 4959):

"Any one who will look over the subject carefully and fairly, especially in the light of the experience in California, must, on the whole, become convinced that the admission of a foreign race so entirely inconsistent with ours, so different from ours in modes and habits of thought, a people that are entirely of a distinct race, kind, quality, and religion, so different in every thing from us not to be allowed to the extent of our trying to absorb that population with the other elements we have got already, some of which are bad enough. We certainly can not expect to absorb that population and make it a part of the great American people."

* Congressional Record, Vol. 17, pages 4950-5100.

manner in which they execute laws. The laboring men of the country have in the *life*, *character*, and *services* of Mr. Sherman the highest guaranty that *their interests will be safe in his hands.*

At the tender age of six years, left fatherless to the care of a widowed mother with eleven children, with limited means, he was soon thrown upon his own resources, and has worked his unaided way, a self-made man, to his high and honorable eminence. At fourteen years of age he became junior rodman in the engineer force engaged in the improvement of the Muskingum River, and so continued for over two years. In this and other positions, which space does not permit to be traced, he became inured to toil, and has never wavered in his sympathy for all in like condition. His private life, his public acts, and all his utterances prove this.

With views so clearly and forcibly expressed, and with a record on great questions so well understood, Mr. Sherman as a candidate will *solidify the Republican party*, give satisfaction to the laboring men of the party, and attract to his support many laboring men who have been tariff Democrats.

His position on labor questions will turn the scale in favor of Republican success in doubtful States like West Virginia, Virginia, Tennessee, New Jersey, and Connecticut, and save the Empire State in the Republican column.

II.

SHERMAN JUSTLY AVAILABLE WITH COLORED VOTERS.

II. MR. SHERMAN *is the leading and most popular candidate in this, that he can carry more votes of colored citizens than any other.*

This is shown by the support given him by colored delegates in the National Convention of 1880 ; by the strong current of opinion in newspapers published by colored citizens ; and is a result of " the logic of events," which proves that he has done as much if not more *good, effective service* than any living American statesman in behalf of human freedom, the protection of the civil and political rights of colored citizens, and their intellectual and moral progress.

The history of his devotion to the rights of the colored race is that

of his manhood life, and *antedates the organization of the Republican party.*
The Missouri Compromise of 1820 solemnly declared that slavery should
never be extended north of thirty-six degrees and thirty minutes north
latitude. The repeal of this by the Kansas-Nebraska act of 1854 was
designed to carry slavery into Kansas, and the "Dred-Scott decision" of
1857 emphasized the purpose avowed in Calhoun's resolutions of February 19, 1847, to carry slavery into *every* Territory of the United States.
Prior to 1855 the two great political parties had been the Whig, with
which Mr. Sherman was allied, and the Democratic. The Freesoil party
had made some progress as a separate party. The repeal by the Democrats in Congress in 1854 of the Missouri Compromise led to a reorgani-
zation of parties. The Whig and Freesoil parties were abandoned; the
great body of the Whigs, Freesoilers, and the anti-slavery Democrats
"fused" in 1854, in Ohio, under the name of the Anti-Nebraska party.
This *fusion* nominated Mr. Sherman, then only thirty-one years of age,
as a candidate for Representative in Congress in the strong Democratic
Richland district, in which he resided, and he was triumphantly elected.
Following this election the Republican party was organized. Its first State
Convention, of which Mr. Sherman was President, was held in Ohio
July 13, 1855. It adopted an anti-slavery platform, and nominated
Salmon P. Chase for Governor, and other candidates for other offices.
Mr. Sherman's speech on that occasion put him in the front rank in
opposition to slavery extension. On July 16th, at a ratification meeting
at Mansfield, he offered resolutions, which were adopted, indorsing the
platform and candidates, and made a speech* which rang through the
nation, as terse, as far-reaching in purpose, and more grand and eloquent
even than Lord Mansfield's immortal decision in the Somerset case,†
whose terms in prose have been translated into the fervid exclam-
ation of Cowper:

> "Slaves can not breathe in England; if their lungs
> Receive our air, that moment they are free:
> They touch our country, and their shackles fall.
> That's noble! and bespeaks a Nation proud." ‡

Then followed the contest in Congress, whether slavery should secure
the fruits of repeal.

---

* He said among other things as to the repeal: "A great outrage has been committed;
a solemn compact broken; the rights of the North have been trampled under foot, and slavery
is about to be extended over free territory. Under these circumstances the friends of freedom
of all parties have come together, forgetting party ties, and stand upon the broad platform
of "No more slave States—no more slave territory."

† 20 State Trials, 2; 6 Ohio St. R. 664.

‡ Birney vs. State, 8 Ohio, 235.

Mr. Sherman first took his seat in the House of Representatives at the opening of its session in December, 1855, when there was a fierce and protracted struggle attending the election of Speaker. On the ninety-ninth ballot he gave his reasons for voting for General Banks, as follows :

" I care not whether he is a member of the American party or not. I have been informed that he is, and I believe that he is ; but I repeat, I care not to what party he belongs. I understand him to take this position—that the repeal of the Missouri Compromise was an act of great dishonor, and that, under no circumstances whatever, will be, if he have the power, allow the institution of human slavery to derive any benefit from that repeal. That is my position. I have been a Whig, but I will yield all party preferences, and will act in concert with men of all parties and opinions who will steadily aid in preserving our Western territories for free labor ; and I say now that I never will vote for a man for Speaker of this House unless he convinces me by his conduct and by his views that he never will, if he has the power to prevent it, allow the institution of slavery to derive any advantage from repealing the compromise of 1820.

A variety of resolutions were introduced, as the balloting for Speaker was continued, propounding interrogatories as to the political opinions of the several candidates. Mr. Sherman finally introduced one which read thus :

"*Resolved,* That the only tests of the opinions of any candidate for public office are his votes and acts ; and that no man ought to occupy the high position of Speaker of this House whose opinions upon important political questions are so unknown that it is necessary to examine him as a witness."

Kansas had meanwhile become a battle-ground between the advocates of slavery from the South and the opponents of it from the free States, each faction hoping to secure the ascendency. A state of violence, amounting to actual civil war, ensued, and numbers were killed in guerrilla contests. Rival State Governments were established, each with its Constitution, Governor, and Legislature, while acts of horrible atrocity were committed by organized bands of "Border Ruffiaus," who roamed about the country plundering and often murdering peaceable and unoffending settlers. The matter became so serious that the House of Representatives passed a resolution, on the 19th of March, authorizing the appointment of a committee of three by the Speaker to inquire into and collect evidence in regard to the troubles in Kansas generally, and particularly in regard to any fraud or force attempted or practiced in relation to any of the elections which had taken place in that Territory.*

° Poore's Life of Sherman, page 10.

Mr. Sherman, in his first term in Congress,* was placed on the committee, and though he was not chairman, yet he wrote the elaborate, exhaustive, and able report which was submitted to the House July 1, 1856.† This, the first great document on the subject ever submitted to Congress by any statesman of the Republican party, secured in its varied results freedom to Kansas, and gave such impetus to the Republican cause as to insure its ascendency to the control of the National Government with the election of Mr. Lincoln in 1860.‡

In the presidential election of 1856, Mr. Sherman supported Colonel John C. Fremont for the Presidency, in opposition to Mr. Buchanan and Mr. Fillmore. To use his own words, he acted with the Republican party, with hundreds of thousands of others, simply because the Republican party resisted the extension but did not seek the abolition of slavery. The election of Mr. Buchanan aroused the free States to their utmost energy of action. He not only was pledged to advance the interests of the slave-holding States by extending that institution in the Territories, but by the acquisition of Cuba. Mr. Sherman stoutly combated the President's views. In reply to an inquiry put to him in the House of Representatives as to carrying slavery into the Territories under the operation of the Constitution, he said: "The Constitution of the United States carries slavery nowhere. It is a local institution, confined within State limits, and goes nowhere except where express law carries it."

Mr. Sherman, while a zealous champion of the rights of the Free States, took also an active part in legislation on a variety of practical questions. In the debate on the submarine telegraph he showed his opposition to monopolies by saying: "I can not agree that our Government should be bound by any contract with any private incorporated company for fifty years; and the amendment I desire to offer will reserve the power to Congress to determine the proposed contract after ten years." In the debate on the tariff bill, with a view to the reduction of the revenue and an increase of the free list, Mr. Sherman said: "The additions to the free list should be of articles not produced in this country, and whose free importation will not compete in any way with the great interests of any section of this country."

---

* House Journal, Part I., 1st and 2d Sessions 34th Congress, pp. 700, 717, 719.

† House Journal, Part II., 1st and 2d Sessions 34th Congress, p. 1143: Reports of Committees, 1st and 2d Sessions 34th Congress, Vol. II., 1855–56; Bronson's Life of Sherman, 82.

‡ See debates on Kansas, Appendix Congressional Globe, 1st Session 34th Congress, p. 1005; Cong. Globe, Part II., 1st Session 34thCongress, 1855–56, p. 1525; speech Dec. 8, 1856, Appendix Congressional Globe, 3d Session 34th Congress, 1856–57; speech Jan. 28, 1858, Congressional Globe, Vol. XXXVI., Part I., 1st Session, 35th Congress, p. 476.

The Kansas question occupied a prominent place in the proceedings of the Thirty-fifth Congress. Mr. Sherman, in an able speech against the admission of the new State into the Union, took the ground that Congress should not recognize the Lecompton or any other constitution that had not been framed by a convention to which the people had delegated full power, and which had not been subsequently submitted to and approved by a popular vote."* He then said:

" In conclusion, allow me to impress the South with two important warnings she has received in her struggle for Kansas. One is, that though her able and disciplined leaders on this floor, aided by executive patronage, may give her the power to overthrow legislative compacts, yet while the sturdy integrity of the Northern masses stands in her way she can gain no practical advantage by her well-laid schemes. The other is, that while she may indulge with impunity the spirit of fillibusterism, or lawless and violent adventure, upon a feeble and distracted people in Mexico and Central America, she must not come in contact with that cool, determined courage and resolution which forms the striking characteristic of the Anglo-Saxon race. In such a contest her hasty and impetuous violence may succeed for a time, but the victory will be short-lived, and leave nothing but bitterness behind. Let us not war with each other; but with the grasp of fellowship and friendship, regarding to the full each other's rights—and let us be kind to each other's faults—let us go hand in hand in securing to every portion of our people their constitutional rights."

In the 35th and 36th Congresses, and subsequently in the Senate, Mr. Sherman supported all the measures which rescued our vast territories from slavery, and gave freedom and equal civil and political rights to all alike, regardless of *race, color,* or *previous condition of servitude.* Among these were the "Wilmot Proviso;" the act to abolish slavery in the District of Columbia; the proclamation of emancipation; the 13th, 14th, and 15th amendments to the Constitution, and the several acts to carry them into effect. He was among the earliest and ablest advocates of enlisting colored men as soldiers.†

When Lee surrendered to Grant at Appomattox in April, 1865, the State governments in operation in the seceded States were those recognizing allegiance to the so-called Confederate Constitution. President Johnson undertook, by proclamation, to reorganize new State governments through conventions of delegates, to be elected by those mainly who had been in rebellion, *excluding colored citizens from all right to vote.* Congress denied the authority of the President to reorganize State gov-

---

* Poore's Life of Sherman, page 13.
† See speech on Militia Bill in Senate, July, 1862.

ernments, claiming that this must be done under its sanction by virtue of that clause of the Constitution which requires Congress to " guarantee to every State in this Union a republican form of government." The House passed a bill, which went to the Senate, and there Mr. Sherman offered a substitute, which over the President's veto became the *first reconstruction act* of March 2, 1867.*

COLORED CITIZENS INDEBTED TO SHERMAN FOR THE RIGHT OF SUFFRAGE.

Thus Mr. Sherman was the author of *the first act ever passed by Congress which gave to colored citizens the right to vote*, and required that the constitution of each of the reorganized States should provide " that the elective franchise shall be enjoyed by all such persons." To this measure, its example, and its *fruits*, and thus to Mr. Sherman, *every colored citizen is indebted for his right to vote.* The credit is his none the less if it be said, if he had not lived, some other might have secured the same result. The same may be said of Grant and Sherman and Sheridan and Logan, and all the great soldiers of the war.

When State governments had been organized under Mr. Sherman's law, the Democratic leaders in the Southern States, or *their followers*, succeeded very largely in depriving colored citizens not only of the privilege of voting, but of civil rights as well. At first the enemies of the colored race sullenly took but little part in the control of these States; in the second stage, by organized " Kuklux Klans," they deprived colored citizens of their rights by intimidation, violence, and murder; and in the third, not yet ended, mainly by fraudulent counts of vote and false election returns, supplemented occasionally by intimidation.†

During this second stage General Grant, then Président, asked Congress to give him enlarged power to protect colored citizens against these outrages. For this purpose the " force bill" was introduced in the 2d Session of the 42d Congress, 1871-72; but was finally defeated.‡

The colored citizens all over the South were earnest in the demand for its passage, and they have never ceased to feel that they were

---

*Globe, Part II., 2d Session 39th Congress, 1866-67, pp. 1450, 1462, 1463, 1468; 14 Vol. Stat. 428.

†The evidence of this is found in more than a hundred volumes of reports to Congress. See Gen. Raum's " Existing Conflict," Washington, 1884.

‡See debates, Congressional Record, 2d Session 42d Congress, 1871-72, referred to in index under title of "Enforcement."

abandoned to a cruel fate by the Republicans in Congress who aided the Democrats in defeating the bill. They thought if military force could be properly employed to save the Government, it might rightfully be used to protect citizens in their rights when all other means failed. *In that crisis, involving their rights and lives, Mr. Sherman stood by them.** In addition to this he is *in advance of all others* in demanding, as he now does, that "in States where it is ascertained that free and orderly elections for Senators and Representatives in Congress can not be had, Congress should assert and exercise its unquestioned power to regulate the times, places, and manner of holding such elections."†

With such a law the Government that gave political rights to the colored race could secure to them their enjoyment.

SHERMAN FAVORS NATIONAL AID TO EDUCATION.

Mr. Sherman is the earnest friend of national aid to education. He has said "the Republican party is in favor of aiding the States in the education of illiterate children by liberal appropriations of public money."‡

---

* On June 1, 1887, Mr. Sherman, in his Springfield (Ill.) speech, said: "I always thought that this bill should have passed," and he quoted Democratic authority—Reverdy Johnson's speech—describing the outrages the bill was designed to prevent, in which he said: " The outrages proved are shocking to humanity ; they admit of neither excuse nor justification; . . they show that the parties engaged were brutes, insensible to the obligations of humanity and religion.'

† This was declared in his speech delivered before the Legislature of Illinois, by request of that body, at Springfield, June 1, 1887, and in a Mansfield interview, June 15, 1887, published in the Cincinnati Enquirer. It was in substance reiterated in his Toledo speech of July 28, 1887. The following is from the Enquirer report of the interview:

"'I would have Congress enact a law fixing the time, manner, and circumstances of electing members of Congress, defining and providing for the rights of every citizen at such an election, and putting it wholly with the Government for the conduct and regulation of congressional elections. In other words, the entire supervision of the election of members of Congress should be with the United States Government.'

"'But is there any warrant for that in the constitution?

"'Clearly ; that principle has been decided by the courts on several occasions, and the Supreme Court has laid down the doctrine unequivocally, and its decisions are in the line of its establishment. With such a statute enforced, there could be no abridgment of the elective franchise, no suppression of ballots in elections concerning the interests of government. Then if communities, or even States, should attempt to deprive citizens of their rights of franchise, the Government could lawfully interfere, put an end to it, and rehabilitate every citizen. With the right to every citizen to cast his vote and have it counted for members of Congress and electors for President clearly established and enforced, the same right at State and local elections would soon enforce itself, although there would be no governmental interference.'

"'Then you would have the same law apply in the choice of Presidential Electors that applied in the election of members of Congress?'

"'Certainly, and why not?'"

‡ Speech before the Legislature of Tennessee, at Nashville, March 24, 1887. He also said: "This is considered an object of the highest public policy, for without intelligence no people can safely be trusted with political power. This is especially true as to the South, where a large population has been converted by the results of the war into citizens with political power. As to these, at any rate, there could be no question that it is the duty of Congress to provide for at least the elements of education. It so happens that on account of the sparsity of population of the South and the abolition of slavery, the proportion of

Mr. Sherman carries his principles into his every-day life. On the 22d of March, 1887, during his tour through the Southern States, a delegation of five leading colored citizens, including preachers and editors, sent him a note to the hotel where he was stopping at Birmingham, Ala., saying that they would like to pay their respects to him "in behalf of the colored people, *as he was an acknowledged leader of their party.*" He invited them to call the next morning at his room. When the morning came they sent him a note, saying they were not allowed by the manager of the hotel to call; and on learning that this was true, Mr. Sherman immediately removed to another hotel, where he received the colored citizens, showing them all the courtesy and attention he could to any others.

Thus Mr. Sherman *has done more* to secure freedom, civil and political rights for the colored people than any living statesman. And he does not weary in well-doing. His views and purposes promise for the future all that any colored citizen can desire. If nominated for the Presidency, they would rally to his support as they would to Lincoln if living. He can carry Virginia, West Virginia, probably also North Carolina, South Carolina, and perhaps other States, which a candidate not acceptable to the colored citizens might lose, and the same may be said of New Jersey, Connecticut, and other Northern States. The Republican party can not afford to surrender a certainty of success. The colored voters are a power which commands respect and attention. and which *duty* will not permit to be ignored. Give them Sherman and they "will preserve the jewel of liberty in the household of its friends."

---

illiterates here is much greater than in the North, where no such conditions have existed, and where the great mass of children have received the elements of education at the expense of the State; and yet Northern Republicans have been willing out of the common treasury to pay to the Southern States a proportion of this money two or three times greater than to the same number of people in the Northern States. In the last Congress the Senate of the United States passed a bill making a large and liberal provision to aid the States in the education of their children. The Democratic party has thus far been able to defeat the proposition. During the last session a Democratic Speaker refused to recognize even Democratic members to test the sense of the House as to this bill. Thus, by the mandate of the Democratic party, not even an opportunity has been presented to take the sense of the House upon the subject."

The philanthropic and able Senator Blair has devoted much time and energy to secure the passage of a bill to aid education in the States, *the object of which has the hearty approval of Senator Sherman.* (Congressional Record, Vol. XV., 1st Session 48th Congress, pp. 2061, 2062, 2039, 2251, 2252, 2691, 2692, 2714.) Mr. Sherman said:

"I think the safety of the National Government demands that we should remove this dark cloud of ignorance that rests upon a portion of the people of the States. Without reproaches to any section, I am willing as one of the Senators of Ohio . . . to vote from the National Treasury a large sum of money this year, and from time to time so long as the necessity exists a liberal sum of money, to aid in the education of the illiterate children of the Southern and Northern States."

III.

SHERMAN ACCEPTABLE TO THE SOUTHERN REPUBLI-CANS—HE CAN SECURE A LARGE CONFEDERATE VOTE—HIS CONSERVATIVE VIEWS.

III. Mr. Sherman *is the leading and most popular candidate in this, that he will command the united support of the Republicans and of many conservative Democrats in the Southern States.*

There is a large body of those men who were in the Confederate service who accept the results of the war; they are ready to unite in all measures to secure "a free ballot and a fair count;" they desire that the *animosities* of the war shall cease, that the "bloody shirt" shall no longer be waved, and that the resources and industries of the South shall be developed.*

Senator Mahone is one of these, and he has declared in favor of Sherman, who, more than any other candidate, is satisfactory to this conservative class. This results from his pacific utterances, from his prominence as an advocate of a protective tariff, and his conservative character.

In his recent Springfield (Ill.) speech Mr. Sherman said:

" I do not wish to utter one word to revive the animosities of the war; that was fought out manfully and bravely by the two contending parties, with such courage as to inspire the respect of each side for the other, and to its logical conclusion of the complete success of the Union cause. All that I ask is that the defeated party will honorably fulfill the terms of their surrender, and that the results of the war may be respected and observed with honor by Confederates, and firmly, but with charity and kindness, by Union soldiers and citizens. For this I appeal alike to Confederate and Union soldiers, to the blue and the gray, so that when

---

* Senator Mahone, of Virginia, it is believed, voiced the opinion and wishes of a large majority of Republicans in most of the Southern States when, after declaring in favor of Sherman's nomination, he said: " In my judgment the country does not possess for the Republican cause a more *available* candidate—certainly no man or statesman of purer or superior qualifications—for the supreme distinction and trust. He is great in self-possession, courage, knowledge, and truth." (Letter to A. L. Conger, Akron, O., May 21, 1887; Cincinnati Commercial Gazette, July 29, 1887.).

passion and prejudice disappear both sides will stand by each other in the improvement and development of our great and united country."

As early as January, 1875, on the Louisiana resolution of Senator Schurz, he said:

"I do with all my heart respond to the peroration of a speech made the other day by the Senator from Georgia (Mr. Gordon) for peace, harmony, and good-will. He says he is heartily sick of all this stirring up of bad passions. So am I. Whatever I can do to secure the rights of the people of Louisiana to *govern themselves* according to law in harmony with the Constitution, and so as to secure them all in life, liberty, and property, this will I surely do.*

And on the 27th of April, 1886, in an address on the "New South," he said:

"We must not be impatient with the New South. . . I see growing up every day the evidences of that feeling that this sectional controversy is at an end. . . The duty of both sections . . is to adopt a policy, approved by the patriotic men of both sections, that will develop the resources, improve the conditions, and advance the interests of the whole people. The North is ready for this consummation."†

These are not isolated utterances.

It was because Mr. Sherman had made a special study of the means of developing the resources of the New South—by the protection of industries, by opening new channels of trade and commerce with the American republics and Brazil, by the protection of her citizens in all their rights, the education of her people, the growth of manufactories, and by peaceful relations among all the people, between all the States, and with foreign nations—that the Legislature of Tennessee invited him to address that body, as he did March 24, 1887, when he avowed all these purposes, alike beneficial to the South and to the great North, whose trade will be enlarged thereby. No such invitation has been extended by any State to any other candidate.

In his Nashville speech he said:

"As to the improvement of the great arteries of commerce traversing or bounding States, as to the improvement of the rivers and harbors of the country, I believe, in common with the Republican party, that it is the duty of Congress, from such money in the treasury not otherwise

---

* Speech in the Senate, January 16 and 22, 1875; and see speech before the Ohio Legislature, January 14, 1886. In the latter he said: "As we recede from the war, its issues and its passions are disappearing from our politics."

† Speech in Metropolitan M. E. Church, Washington City, April 27, 1886.

appropriated, from time to time to make proper appropriations for national improvements. You have in Tennessee, it is said, the greatest length of navigable rivers of any State. The improvement of the Mississippi, Tennessee, and Cumberland rivers is of the greatest importance to your internal and external commerce. Yet your State can not make these improvements. Such attempts have been made by many of the States, and have been abandoned. One of the great objects of the formation of the Government was to secure such improvements for commerce. The great cities of the country think that all rivers and harbors are unimportant except their own, and yet the commerce of the Ohio and Mississippi rivers is much greater in quantity and value than the commerce of the United States with foreign nations. No portion of the public expenditure is more prolific of benefit, or is more carefully disbursed than that expended by the Engineer Corps in the improvement of our rivers and harbors. If President Cleveland had ever been west of Buffalo, he would never have pocketed the river and harbor bill. I believe also that it is wise public policy to erect suitable public buildings to carry on the business of the country, wherever the amount of business will justify such an expenditure. .... The Republican party . . is now prepared to open commercial relations with our neighboring countries—Mexico, the Dominion · of Canada, Brazil, and the South American republics. It proposes to increase our business relations with all these neighboring countries by the establishment of lines of steamships, by the extension of American railroads into and through them, by commercial regulations that will be liberal and just to our friendly neighbors."

His nomination means an end to the Democratic "Solid South," with Republican success in Virginia, West Virginia, Tennessee, and probably other Southern States.

IV.

SHERMAN, THE GREATEST LIVING FINANCIER, HAS THE CONFIDENCE OF BUSINESS MEN.

IV. MR. SHERMAN *is the leading and most popular candidate in this, that as the author of currency, revenue, and public debt measures in the Senate, and their execution as Secretary of the Treasury, he has rendered greater services on these subjects than any other statesman, and has more than any other candidate the confidence of the "business men" of the country.*

If it can be said that any one great quality more than any other is required in a President *for the next term*, it is that *he shall be a great financier*—not for one class, but *for the benefit of all.* The history of nations is largely that of war and finances. Fortunately, with a conservative President for the next term, the business of the country will be safe from war; the great question will be *finance*—revenue and currency.

The whole country recognizes the necessity of the *revision of our revenue system.*

SHERMAN CAN DEAL WITH "THE SURPLUS"—RELIEF FROM TAXATION.

President Cleveland, in his annual message of December 6, 1887, said:

"The amount of money annually exacted, through the operation of present laws, from the industries and necessities of the people largely exceeds the sum necessary to meet the expenses of the Government. . . . . . . On the 30th day of June, 1885, the excess of revenues over public expenditures, after complying with the annual requirement of the Sinking Fund act, was $17,859,735.84. During the year ending June 30, 1886, such excess amounted to $49,105,545.20, and during the year ending June 30, 1887, it reached the sum of $55,567,849.54. . . . . While the expedients thus employed to release to the people the money lying idle in the treasury served to avert immediate danger, our surplus revenues have continued to accumulate, the excess for the present year amounting on the 1st day of December to $55,258,701.19, and estimated to reach the sum of $113,000,000 on the 30th of June next, at which date it is expected that this sum, added to prior accumulations, will swell the surplus in the treasury to $140,000,000."

The responsibility for this has been stated by high Democratic authority—the New York World, of September 5, 1887—as follows:

" For *twelve years* now the Democratic party has been demanding a reduction of the war taxes, and pledging itself to stop the surplus. For the greater part of this time it has had control of the lower House of Congress, *in which revenue measures must originate* [Const. U. S., Art. I., Sec. 7], and *not once has it passed a bill through that House reducing the taxes.* In the last two Congresses, though having a large majority, it was unable even to secure consideration for the subject. . . . If the Democratic leaders wish the country to believe that they mean to stop the surplus by reducing the taxes, they must pass a bill for that purpose. *Talk will not do.*"*

After the close of the war, and with a large reduction in the national debt, it became necessary to lessen the revenues by reducing taxation. Accordingly Congress, with a Republican majority in both branches, passed three acts of July 14, 1870, June 6, 1872, and March 3, 1883— voted against by the Democratic members—largely reducing internal revenue taxation, and so adjusting tariff duties as to diminish revenue from that source. Much of this legislation was secured through the agency of Mr. Sherman as Chairman of the Senate Finance Committee.

As early as September 24, 1884, Mr. Sherman, with his usual sagacity, foreseeing the necessity of further reductions, in a speech at Columbus, O., on the " Distribution of the Surplus," said:

" I am among those who have always favored the gradual and careful reduction of taxation, so that the surplus revenue may be sufficient only to meet the expenses of the Government economically administered, and a further sum . . to cover the sinking fund and have some leeway against a reduction of receipts."

And referring to the act of March 3, 1883, he said:

" In the main the general features of that law were wise and useful. It repealed all the [internal revenue] taxes on proprietary medicines, on bank-checks, on friction matches, and a multitude of onerous and offensive taxes. . . It *largely reduced* the tax on an important agricultural staple—tobacco."

* See Sherman's speech, Nashville, March 21, 1887; speech at Columbus, September 24, 1884; speech in Senate, December 9, 1886; Congressional Record, Vol. XVIII , p. 65.

He added that he felt bound " to say in candor that the reductions of [tariff] taxation . . have not always been wise," and he vigorously maintained the necessity of giving full protection to all American industries.

Since the act of 1883 no further reduction of taxation has been made, because the Democratic party, having a majority in the House of Representatives, failed to pass any bill; and although the Senate can, under the Constitution, " propose or concur with amendments" on such bills, yet " all bills for raising revenue shall *originate* in the House." (Constitution, Art. I., Sec. 7.)

In his Wilmington (Ohio) speech, September 15, 1887, Mr. Sherman said:

" The money of the people should not be withdrawn from the channels of circulation except to meet proper national expenditures, and when collected it should be paid out as rapidly as its proper application will admit. Whenever the revenues are in excess of the public wants the taxes should be repealed or modified. This duty has been frequently performed by the Republican party. Since the close of the war, taxes have been repealed or remitted [by three acts] that would have yielded $250,000,000 a year. The last reduction in 1883 was made by a Republican Congress of more than $50,000,000 of yearly revenue, unwisely in some particulars, but still a reduction of revenue."

The proper mode of reducing revenues has been in part pointed out by Mr. Sherman. An "interview" with him on June 15, 1887, is thus reported:

"' How should Congress improve the financial situation?'

"' By reducing taxation and preventing the accumulation of an unnecessary surplus in the treasury. If we go on at the rate of accumulating over $100,000,000 annually of useless and unnecessary revenue, and locking it up in the treasury, all our industrial and commercial interests will be jeopardized.'

"' But how can taxation be reduced?'

"' By a revision of the tariff and modification of the internal revenue laws.'

"' Will there be a revision and modification of the tariff laws?'

"' There will doubtless be a reduction on numerous items.'

"' Where do you think the reduction should be applied?'

"' I think that there should be a decided reduction in the tariff on sugar, and then a bounty should be paid on American sugar sufficiently generous to secure the production of all the sugar in the United States that our people may consume. We have the best soil in the world for the sugar-beet and sorghum-cane, covering almost limitless areas, and we have a larger area adapted to the cultivation of West India cane, as in Louisiana. We ought to produce all the sugar we consume, and we may readily do so by a judicious tariff and liberal bounty to producers. It is the same as it was in regard to iron and steel and other products. We used to think that we had to depend upon foreign countries for these. Why, since I was a man grown we got all our planes and saws and tools of all kinds from England. But by fostering our home manufactories we now supply all our home needs and go into the markets of the world.'

"The Senator then went into a long eulogy of the beauties of a protective tariff: how it has been making the workingmen happy and contented all these years."

And in his Toledo speech, July 28, 1887, he indorsed the Ohio Republican Platform, declaring that, if too much revenue be collected, "we demand that the *first step* in the reduction thereof shall be the abolition of the internal tax upon American-grown tobacco." This is an article consumed by nearly all our adult male population, and, when revenue therefrom is unnecessary, no reason exists why the great body of the people of moderate means should be burdened with the tax and a product of our agricultural industry be subject to an onerous imposition. Yet President Cleveland, in his recent message, referring to the internal revenue tax on tobacco, beer, and spirits, says:

" The internal revenue tax is levied upon the consumption of tobacco and spirituous and malt liquors. It must be conceded that *none* of the things subject to internal revenue taxation are, strictly speaking, necessaries; there appears to be no *just* complaint of this taxation by the consumers of these articles, and there seems to be nothing so well able to bear the burden without hardship to any portion of the people."

Thus the President declares the Democratic policy to be to *retain the tax on tobacco* in order thereby to cut down a protective tariff; Mr. Sherman would remove the tax on tobacco as unnecessary, as oppressive, and as a *means of retaining the protective features* of the tariff laws. President Cleveland would retain the tax on spirits and beer, and apply them in paying ordinary expenses of the Government, to cut down the protective features of the tariff; Mr. Sherman would retain the tax on spirits *used as a beverage only* while needed for revenue, when it could be left for the States, each for itself, as a proper subject for taxation. The States could not probably agree on a uniform system of taxing all spirits produced by distillation, as spirits produced in some States are largely consumed in others; but a tax on its *consumption* within any State can be made to relieve local taxation, and for the support of common schools, now a severe burden upon property.

TREATIES WITH OTHER NATIONS AS TO SILVER—LEGISLATION IN RELATION TO COIN AND CURRENCY.

The next administration must treat with other nations as to *silver*, and legislation may be required on the same subject, and as to *greenbacks*, *national bank notes*, and *gold and silver certificates*, all circulating as money. If some other nations will not exchange their commodities for our silver, it may be necessary for us to *trade with nations that will*. These are among the great subjects for the next administration.

Mr. Blaine has said that Mr. Sherman "established a financial reputation not second to any man in our history."* This can not be said of any other living statesman, much less of any other candidate for the Presidency. The compliment is more than deserved.

FINANCIAL CONDITION IN 1861—CURRENCY THEN UNSOUND.

The Republican party came into power March 4, 1861. The credit of the Government had become so low that in January, 1861, a Democratic Secretary of the Treasury "suggested to Congress, as a financial resource, that the several States be asked, as security for any money the Government might find it necessary to borrow, to pledge the deposits received by them from the Government under the act for the distribution of the surplus revenues in 1836."† Buchanan's administration sold six per cent twenty-year Government bonds at an average rate of $89.10 per one hundred dollars. The treasury was bankrupt. ‡

One of the facts of our history is that Democratic administrations have rarely ever been able, in executing *their own policy*, to raise the requisite national revenues. Republican administrations have never failed in this respect, and thereby they have surpassed other nations. The chief struggle with the statesmen of Europe is to obtain sufficient revenue; our chief difficulty is to reduce ours to the limits of our wants —a difficulty which Mr. Sherman can solve, but which a Democratic administration can not.

---

* Blaine, Vol. II., p. 611,

† Sherman's letter, September 25, 1878, to Hon. C. H. Grosvenor.

‡ Boutwell's book, "Why am I a Republican?" (p. 65) says the balance in the treasury January 1, 1861, was $2,283,220, "a sum inadequate for the safe management of a first-class bank."

The total coin in the country in 1860 was $214,000,000; total currency —State bank paper—$207,102,477.* Forty years of Democratic rule had failed to establish a safe paper currency. In this condition of affairs the Republican party came into power, and with it a Southern civil war, which required an expenditure of $6,189,929,908 from July 1, 1861, to June 30, 1879.†

Our people could give a million of soldiers to save the Republic, but who among all the great financiers could devise the means to raise that vast sum of money and displace the hazardous paper currency with one finally to become the best in the world?

SHERMAN LARGELY THE AUTHOR OF OUR WHOLE FINANCIAL SYSTEM, WHICH INSURED OUR SUCCESS IN SUPPRESSING THE REBELLION.

As member or chairman of the Finance Committee of the Senate Mr. Sherman was mainly the author of the acts of Congress which, by *customs duties* ‡ and *internal taxes*, brought in large revenues; the *acts authorizing greenbacks*, which helped to supplement our resources; the *loan acts*, under which money was borrowed on Government bonds, and under which the largest bonded indebtedness was, on January 7, 1866, $2,739,491,745, and the highest rate of interest ever paid was $7\frac{3}{10}$ per cent; the *national bank acts*, which by levying a tax of ten per cent on local bank circulation wiped it out, and more than supplied its place by national currency; the *refunding acts*, by which three per cent Government bonds have reached a premium; the acts from time to time *reducing internal taxation and duties;* the acts *relating to coinage and gold and silver certificates*, which constitute a part of our currency; and the great *resumption act* of January 14, 1875, which brought resumption January 1, 1879. The loan acts themselves have been compiled in a volume.

What have been the fruits? Funds were raised to pay the vast expenditure mentioned; the war was prosecuted to a successful issue: the *credit* of the Government was improved in the very agonies of flagrant war, almost without the aid of foreign capital, and in spite of

---

* Finance Report, 1886.

† Senate Executive Document, No. 206, 2d Session 46th Congress.

‡ The so-called "Morrill" tariff act of March 2, 1861, consists of an amendment offered to the bill by Mr. Sherman, which embraced the principal protective provisions agreed on by Messrs. Morrill, Sherman, and other leading friends of the measure.

foreign hostility,* and now it is better than that of any nation on the globe. All these great measures were so wisely perfected that the people prospered financially, and grew in wealth even during the war, as ever since.

This is the only instance in the world's history where such a result has followed under similar circumstances. And now we have an aggregate of coin and currency of $1,747,331,525, with revenues too abundant, and our national debt, exclusive of greenbacks and less available cash in the treasury, only $908,788,275. The chief struggle with other nations is to obtain sufficient revenue; ours is to reduce it to the limit of our wants. The reduction of the public debt in England and France has been merely nominal for many years, and ultimate payment, if ever made, is for the distant centuries; the reduction of our debt is so rapid, the only danger is it may come before we can adapt ourselves to the transition.

In 1873 Jay Cooke & Co. suspended. This produced alarm, and panic followed, but not bankruptcy. In former financial panics people ran upon banks to obtain coin for paper which they feared was not good. In 1873 depositors called for payment of money they knew to be good. This soon passed away.

SHERMAN'S GREAT RESUMPTION ACT—HIS SUCCESS IN EXECUTING IT.

Early in the war the local banks, then existing under State authority, *suspended specie payments.* With the character of the banks which then furnished the only paper money circulation this was inevitable. Of course during the war it was not possible to raise *coin* to conduct all of its vast operations; and following the war, for a period it was only just that the immense private indebtedness contracted on an inconvertible money basis of high prices, and much of the public indebtedness, including a vast amount unfunded, should be discharged with currency substantially of the same value as that on which liabilities were incurred. But no real statesman ever supposed or desired that irredeemable paper should be the permanent currency of any country; history is too full of the evidence of its evils to permit this. Accordingly Mr. Sherman, in the Senate, *gave us the great resumption act* of January 14, 1875, which, with the wisdom of true statesmanship, provided the means of

---

* Henry Clewes in the New York North American Review, October, 1887, pages 413-418.

gradually accumulating coin for resumption by the Government on its
"greenback" issues, and of securing its consummation not immediately,
but with regularly increasing value in currency, approximating that of
coin, during a period of about four years. This brought resumption January
1, 1879, contrary to the predictions of many eminent but less
sagacious and farseeing statesmen than Mr. Sherman.

Doubleday has written the Financial History of England during and
subsequent to her great wars with Napoleon, including resumption on
May 1, 1821, under Sir Robert Peel's act of 59 George III., c. 78, after
a suspension of specie payments, commencing in 1797. Resumption was
accomplished *by withdrawing nearly all the paper money from circulation,*
and this brought utter ruin upon all the debtor class, and to most of the
industries of England. It will require a greater than Doubleday to
write our Financial History from 1860 to our resumption on January 1,
1879, and nothing less will do justice to Mr. Sherman.

Mr. Sherman's resumption act did *not reduce the volume of currency.*
It was said in August, 1879, "instead of that the volume of paper currency
outstanding is still $710,095,968, and is increasing, . . . and
provision is made by existing law for increasing the currency by the
issue of national bank notes whenever the business will justify and
demand their issue."*

The statesmanship of our resumption surpassed that of England's
greatest financier. The statesmanship of France was unequal to the task
of resumption in her greatest issue of paper, and the "assignats" were
finally repudiated.

And added to the services of Mr. Sherman, in connection with these
acts mentioned, is the fact that as Secretary of the Treasury he achieved
the crowning success of perfecting the work of resumption, and of
refunding the bonds at a lower rate of interest than ever before in the
history of the country.

THE NATIONAL BANKING SYSTEM—SHERMAN'S WORK— ITS SUPERIORITY OVER ALL OTHER SYSTEMS— AMENDMENTS NEEDED.

The *national banking system*—born of the necessities of the war—still
survives. It has accomplished and is accomplishing the threefold pur-

---

*Sherman's Steubenville speech, August 20, 1879, and he said: "And gold and silver
coin . . . is in circulation, or is held in reserve in lieu of circulation, to the amount of
$332,443,947, thus showing an aggregate circulation of $1,042,339,915, or $21.11 per inhabitant,'

poses of acting as national fiscal agents, of furnishing a currency for the people, and as the best means yet devised of receiving deposits and making discounts. This is so because of the securities it affords for absolute safety, and because all its operations are subject to periodical examinations to guard against insolvency, fraud, or wrong upon all interested therein. No Democratic National Convention has ventured to suggest an improvement or demand its destruction. But efforts have been made in Congress by Democratic members to secure the repeal of the ten per cent prohibitory tax on State bank circulation, thus to return to the "States' Rights" system of local bank issues, with all their evils, and other hostile legislation has often been proposed and attempted.

These banks furnish a currency from which no man ever did or ever can lose a dollar while the Government survives and maintains its honor. The system is better than that of the Bank of England, or any other established in any country since the first *banco* was organized, under the title of Chamber of Loans, in 1171. The national banks have furnished, and under proper legislation will continue to furnish, a currency adequate for all the wants of the country.*

In securing the national banks the statesmanship of Mr. Sherman exceeds that of all those of all nations through seven centuries of time, and Japan and other governments have certified to the verity of this by copying and adopting his system.

But it must not be supposed the system has ceased to require the care of Congress, under the recommendations of such able financiers as Mr. Sherman, in at least *three* respects :

1. *Taxation.* The banks are taxed, under State authority, higher than any other species of property. High taxation compels them to keep up a higher rate of discount on loans than would be otherwise charged. To add *unnecessary* national taxation is alike unwise and unjust. On this subject Mr. Sherman was reported in an interview as follows :

" ' Would you favor the abolition of the tax on bank circulation ?'

" ' No, I would not. The tax used to be two per cent. Then Congress, by legislation, reduced it one per cent. I would favor a reduction of this tax to one half of one per cent, but I believe in keeping a tax.' "

---

* At the close of 1886 our money was: gold coin, $406,700,000; gold certificates, $131,174,245; silver certificates, $115,977,675; silver dollars, $236,815,484; fractional silver, $70,000,000; national bank notes, $311,699,451; greenbacks, $346,681,016; or a total of $1,619,047,871. The treasury statement includes other items—fractional currency, State bank notes, etc.—and makes the circulation in all $1,747,331,525.

With a conceded necessity for reduction of national taxation, why should banks be made to suffer unnecessary burdens?

2. *The amount of circulation allowed on Government bonds deposited in the national treasury as security for circulation.* The only bonds now available are the four and four-and-a-half per cents. These command a premium of from twenty to twenty-eight per cent. With only ninety per cent of the par value of these now allowed to banks for circulation, it has ceased to be remunerative. Many banks have sold their bonds and reduced their circulation; and if the price of bonds advances there is danger of a contraction of the currency prejudicial to the business of the country. In the same interview above mentioned Mr. Sherman is thus reported:

" First the Senator dwelt upon the necessity of some relief for the national banks.

" ' What would you suggest, Senator?' I asked.

" ' I have a plan,' he said, ' or rather plans, of relief, which I think equitable and fair. You will observe that the national bank circulation is being contracted just as our country is growing. This should not be, because the system is an index of the growth of the country, and adapts itself to its growth. I am in favor of letting the banks do business upon the four and four-and-a-half per cent bonds now outstanding. But in order to equalize the burden upon the banks, because of the high rate of premium at which these bonds are held, I would give them circulation up to the face value of their bonds. This would increase the circulation $30,000,000. I would even go further. I would issue the banks circulation up to the market value of their bonds, and have that value fixed once each year. As a matter of fact and history, the price of these bonds has always advanced, and never depreciated.' "*

And why is not this plan both just and safe? The bonds can never go below par. The interview proceeds:

" ' Would you favor the issue of a two per cent perpetual bond?'

" ' No, I would not vote for it. I do not think it would be wise policy to increase the bonded debt of the country solely for the benefit of the national banks. I am a friend of the national banking system. To issue such a bond, however, would be for the Government to ask the people to loan it money when it had more money than it could get out. The banks themselves, I do not think, would favor such a bond. They would hardly invest their money at two per cent to acquire bonds as a security for circulation when they could loan it at six per cent. Again, it would not satisfy the people as a safe deposit of security for circulation. The banks need relief, and ought to have it. If we give them circulation

---

* See bill "to provide for the issue of circulation to national banking associations," December 4, 1883, Cong Record, Vol. XV., pp. 12, 425.

up to the face value of their bonds instead of ninety per cent as now, they will be relieved. If we give them circulation up to the market value of their bonds, the existing conditions of trouble will be, I think, entirely swept away.'" *

3. *What shall be the banking system when the Government bonds shall be so reduced in amount by payment as no longer to furnish sufficient basis for circulation?* This is not a question of *immediate* concern, and yet its answer can not be delayed until danger is upon us. Who so skillful in preparing the way to avert dangers as the great financier who has encountered and surmounted vastly greater questions and dangers than this?

In all the elements of great financial ability and great financial achievements, Mr. Sherman has no superior in the world's history. No man in the presidential office ever won so high distinction by any civil service as Mr. Sherman has done in the Senate and as Secretary of the Treasury. When financial questions present the great work of the next administration, can any citizen doubt whether gratitude, duty, and interest do not require us to place at the helm the world's greatest living financier?

If he be nominated for the Presidency, *every business man* of the whole country will feel secure. The dealers in farm products—cattle, swine, sheep, horses, wheat, corn, cotton, and wool—the merchants, manufacturers, traders, and shippers—the whole people will rally to his support as they will to that of no other man. They will not be disturbed by visions of war, by hazardous experiments, or by injudicious legislation.

THE GERMANS FAVOR SHERMAN.

The Germans have been distinguished as the advocates of sound, honest money. In the contest for resumption they—Democrats and Republicans alike—espoused the policy of Mr. Sherman. If he be the candidate for President, he can carry enough German Democrats in New

* The veteran Democratic correspondent, W. C. McBride, in the Cincinnati Enquirer, December 2, 1886, has the candor to say:

"In his own house Senator Sherman is a cheery host. His greeting is more cordial than emphatic. He is never demonstrative, but rather inviting and assuring. The Senator ages gracefully. He does not look to-day older than his appearance indicated ten years ago, save that his whiskers have donned the suit tinge of gray and are kept closely cut to the chin No one will gainsay Senator Sherman's knowledge of our financial and economic system. Among the few who have made it a passionate study he stands out like the tall oak. Four years' experience, too, as the Secretary of the Treasury have made him familiar with the very minutiæ of our finance. None better than he is familiar with our national debt, for he led the hosts who conceived it, and then subsequently executed the laws which led us successfully to the resumption of specie payments. From the outset of the conversation I had with the Senator it gravitated naturally to fiscal questions."

York, New Jersey, Connecticut, Indiana, and other States to turn the scale in his favor, and *secure Republican success.** Can it be said with certainty that any other candidate will secure this vote ? Shall the certainty of success be imperiled?

---

*On this subject the following is strong evidence (translated from *Der Republikaner*, New York, August 6, 1887):

"John Sherman is not only the strongest candidate for the Ohio Republicans, and recognized as their foremost leader, but he is likewise the strongest candidate in other States, viz.: New York, Indiana, Connecticut, New Jersey, Virginia, and Kentucky—all of them doubtful, and in the last presidential election 'Democratic' States. Among the German element Mr. Sherman has thousands upon thousands of warm friends and admirers, that appreciate and honor his record as a financier and statesman, and whom no party considerations could prevent from giving him their support as the right man in the presidential office. For eight years past Mr. Sherman has been America's statesman par excellence in the eyes of the German-Americans, and his nomination in 1880 and 1884 would have been of more benefit to the party and to the country than were the nominations that were made by the Republican party. The State of New York, which cast the deciding vote in 1884, and will do it again in 1888, can be won by John Sherman's nomination, because the German-horn citizens of New York would support him almost to a man. The Socialists, Anarchists, and Nihilists among the Germans are not included in this estimate, for these would under no circumstances vote for Sherman, or any other candidate of either party. But the German artisans, industrials, retail dealers, tradesmen, and wholesale merchants, who have "taken root" in the soil of America and become proprietors, and identified themselves with the United States as their home and country, these are the men that could and will give the decisive votes for John Sherman in this State. As in New York, it is likewise in other States where the German element predominates among adopted citizens, and the doubtful States of New Jersey, Indiana, and Connecticut could once more be made to fall into line with a solid Republican North in the lead of John Sherman as the Republican candidate. Virginia and Kentucky are both disputable States, and in each of them John Sherman's name stands higher than that of any one of the Republican leaders. The Ohio Republican Convention has discovered the true road to victory, with John Sherman as the nominee of the Republicans, and it is to be fervently hoped that the Republican Conventions of other States soon to follow will fall into line and second the motion of the Ohio Republicans before the people."

One of the closest political observers and sagacious journalists—Murat Halstead—after a personal survey of the field in New York, and writing from that city, in the Cincinnati Commercial Gazette of December 14, 1887, says:

"It is well known that one of the elements of Republican strength in the Ohio cities is the fullness of German information about financial achievements and the strong German sense as to sound money principles, and the general confidence that German citizens feel in the national and scientific statesmanship of John Sherman. The Germans know pretty well what Sherman has done, and like him and confide in him for it, and they go to him and for him as a man whose character and history would lend an exceptional dignity and give an impressive force to his candidacy. As this has been a distinct help in Ohio, why not in New York? The question is one of comprehensive importance, and it can not be discussed too much or too soon. Well, the claim made by the friends of John Sherman, who press him for the Presidency on the ground that he is the strongest candidate for New York, is that twenty thousand German voters would turn to him who have latterly been voting the Democratic ticket. There are about forty thousand characteristically German voters in this State, and not more than eight or at most ten thousand have adhered steadily to the Republicans. It is claimed that with Sherman in the field not more than ten thousand of the forty thousand Germans would stick to the Democrats."

And his letter in the Commercial Gazette of December 11th says:

"It is said that even Carl Schurz, who, as may be remembered, served in the Cabinet of Hayes with Sherman, would turn up a Sherman man and give him immense assistance; but the rumor lacks, so far as I am informed, any thing like personal corroboration. I do but speak of the things that are in the air—the rumors that are in the winds that blow."

V.

MR. SHERMAN IN FAVOR OF AN ADEQUATE AMERICAN COMMERCIAL MARINE.

V. MR. SHERMAN *is an available candidate in this, that he will command the united support of those interested in the protection and growth of the American Commercial Marine.*

Thomas Jefferson said that "agriculture, manufactures, commerce, and navigation constitute the four pillars of our prosperity." His school of politicians has not always given support to any of these pillars. Mr. Sherman has done more to erect and support the first three than any living statesman. He has been, and is, in full accord with every measure to erect and support the last named; he has co-operated with Senator Fry and ex-Governor Dingley,* member of the House of Representatives, and others who have rendered valuable services in this connection; and if elected President, would give all the power of his administration to protect, encourage, increase, and maintain the American Merchant Marine until ours would be surpassed by that of no other nation.

In 1856 our mercantile marine "approached equality with that of England in tonnage."† The "change from sail to steam," from wood to iron, and dread of and destruction by the British-built cruisers during our civil war, have left us with a commercial marine far inferior to that of other great nations. The result is that our people are paying probably $115,000,000 a year to alien ship-owners for carrying freights to and from our country; and the other nations have a vast advantage in scouring the commerce of the world. American bacon, cheese, butter, and other products are carried to London, stamped as British products, shipped at a profit to South America, and there exchanged for products returned to the United States, with a profit to be paid by our citizens. Congress has imposed discriminating duties against foreign freights in foreign ships, which secure the coasting and lake trade to our own vessels.‡

---

* The services of these and other members of Congress have been of great value.

† Blaine's second volume, p. 611.

‡ Act of Congress of June 26, 1884, 23 U. S. Statutes, 53.

Among the means suggested for securing an adequate supply of American ships, and the carrying trade for them with foreign countries, now so fully monopolized by foreign ships, are liberal appropriations by Congress for carrying mails by American steamship lines; discriminating duties against freights in foreign bottoms; bounties on ship-building; an increase in naval vessels and their use in carrying mails, etc.; exemption of American ships from local taxation;* commercial treaties and friendly relations with Mexico, the South American States, China, Japan, and other countries; the improvement of our rivers and harbors, and such other measures as may be found adequate and expedient. †

There is an organization known as "The Shipping' and Industrial League," whose purpose is to make the restoration and increase of our marine and naval power a leading political issue.   This policy of increase has been indorsed by the recent Republican State Convention in Pennsylvania.

Mr. Sherman is in full sympathy with this policy of commercial development.   He regards it as one to be speedily and effectually made the subject of legislation and treaty stipulations.‡   As early as March 7, 1871, he introduced into the Senate "a bill to facilitate commerce between the United States and China and Japan, and the countries of Asia."   On December 11, 1883, he introduced a bill for the encouragement of closer commercial relationship, and in the interest of and the perpetuation of peace between the United States and the Republics of

---

*See pamphlet, "Views of William Lawrence, of Ohio," published in 1882 by the New York National Chamber of Industry and Trade, p. 10.

†William W. Bates, Esq., editor of the Inland Lloyd's Register, of Buffalo, has discussed the whole subject with great ability in articles published in various papers.   The Marine Journal of New York has done the same.   In its number of December 3, 1887, is a draft of a bill for the consideration of Congress, proposing an appropriation "to any vessel, whether sail or steam, built and owned wholly in the United States, engaged in the foreign trade, the sum of thirty cents per registered ton for each one thousand miles sailed, and *pro rata* for any less distance."

‡ Reference has been already made to the Nashville speech, declaring in favor of opening "commercial relations with our neighboring countries—Mexico, the Dominion of Canada, Brazil, the South American Republics, etc."

Mr. Sherman, in his Springfield (Ill.) speech, June 1, 1887, said:

" Liberal measures should be adopted to increase our trade, to *establish lines of steamships*, to improve postal facilities, to make commercial treaties, and to invite a friendly conference with the American Republics and the Dominion of Canada.   But this has met with no favor with the Democratic party."

In his Wilmington (Ohio) speech, September 15, 1887, he said:

" The opposition by the Democratic party to other just and proper subjects of expenditure, especially for suitable provisions for carrying the mail into foreign ports, for the improvement of the navy, for the coast defense, is in harmony with the general dogmas of the party about the powers of the National Government.   Our flag floating upon the seas, our ships carrying commerce to foreign ports, the protection of particular harbors, and the construction of railroads seem to be contrary to the resolutions of '98 and to the Democratic platform.   Indeed, I know of no act or measure of this administration that tends in any way to the extension of our commerce at home or abroad, to the development of our country, or to promote the business and prosperity of our people."

Mexico, Central America, and the Empire of Brazil." On February 8, 1886, he introduced a bill on the same subject. He is now Chairman of a Joint Committee of the two Houses of Congress in regard to the Exposition proposed to be held in Washington for the purpose of more intimate relations with the South American States. He is also Chairman of the Committee on Foreign Relations, having charge of many of these subjects.

If he be made President, his motto on this subject will be, "Don't give up the ship." The whole country is interested in it: the farmer and manufacturer for a larger market for their products; our hardy seamen for a wider field of employment; the North, that its commerce may be extended; the South, for the same reason, and that her timber may be utilized in ship-building, and ship-yards be multiplied within her borders.

VI.

SHERMAN WILL COMMAND THE CORDIAL SUPPORT OF THE SOLDIERS OF THE UNION ARMY.

VI. MR. SHERMAN *is an available candidate in this, that he will command the cordial support of the soldiers of the Republic.*

Mr. Sherman, while a member of the House of Representatives, in March, 1861, was elected to the Senate of the United States, and took his seat as Senator March 23, 1861. It was not until the attack on Fort Sumter, in April, 1861, that a civil war was regarded inevitable. The Senate having adjourned before this event, Mr. Sherman was on his way home when the first proclamation of Mr. Lincoln calling for 75,000 troops was issued. In the latter part of April two Ohio regiments were ordered to Philadelphia. Mr. Sherman joined them at Harrisburg, and there tendered his services to General Patterson, who appointed him aid-de-camp without pay, and he served in this capacity until the extra session of Congress in July. After the adjournment of this session of Congress, Mr. Sherman, under the authority of Governor Dennison, recruited on his own plan, and largely *at his own expense*, two regiments of infantry, a squadron of cavalry, and a battery of artillery, comprising over 2,300 men. He went to Washington at the meeting of Congress in December, intending to resign his seat as Senator, and offer his services in the army, but changed his purpose at the request of President Lincoln and Secretary Chase, who desired him to remain in the Senate on the ground that he could there "be of more service to the Union cause." *

The suppression of the rebellion required brave, patriotic men, and it also required "the sinews of war"—money. It is an error to suppose that the public debt at any time represented fully the cost of the rebellion. The total "expenditures growing out of the war" from July 1, 1861, to June 30, 1879, were $6,189,920,908; † yet there then remained unpaid of this vast sum a public debt of only $2,249,567,482. No nation in the world's history ever raised so large a sum, and paid off so much of it within the same period. To Mr. Sherman, more than any other man in public life, belongs the credit of this unexampled performance. The measures in Congress, devised and carried through by his agency and aid, fed and clad and paid our soldiers, and furnished the means which brought the war to a successful issue, and has since paid their well-earned and richly-deserved pensions. In hands less competent than those of Mr. Sherman the defeat and fall of the Republic might have been written. For these services he has claims upon the gratitude and the votes of soldiers. *He is in full accord with them in all they ask,* in the way of pensions and otherwise. Chief among their requests is, that Congress will "repeal the restrictions limiting arrearages of pensions to applications made prior to July 1, 1880, and allowing all persons to claim pensions from the date of disability without respect to the time of filing their application." He is in favor of the repeal, and made an earnest and able speech to secure it in the Senate, January 27, 1887. This only reiterated sentiments he expressed in a speech at Mt. Gilead, O., two years earlier, and reaffirmed in a speech at Wilmington, O., September 15, 1887.‡ And on the 5th of January, 1887, he introduced a bill in the Senate extending the principle

* Poore's Life of Sherman, p. 22; Sherman's speech at Shelby, August 21, 1884.

† Senate Ex. Doc. No. 206, 2d Session 46th Congress. Letter Sherman, Secretary of the Treasury.

‡ In this he said:

"With an overflowing treasury the President has prevented by vetoes or by withholding his signature the application of money to most important purposes. They do not know how to reduce the revenue or increase expenditure. I need not refer to the vetoes of small pension bills, for they were trivial in amount, and such as I believe no President of the United States before would have thought it his duty to veto; nor to the dependent mentioned, so as to grant arrears of pensions from the date of disability to soldiers who lost a limb.

He voted for the "dependent pension bill," and others which Cleveland vetoed.. He voted for the law which requires a preference to be given to *soldiers* in making appointments to office; he faithfully executed it when Secretary of the Treasury, and as President would not permit its evasion, as under Cleveland's administration.*

Both before and during the war he was in constant correspondence with his illustrious brother—General W. T. Sherman—and fully shared with him in his devotion to the Union, and the necessity of maintaining the authority of the National Government by force of arms. This correspondence extends through the war, embracing almost every battle or chief event from the time that General Sherman left his position as Military Instructor in Louisiana before the commencement of the war to its close. This correspondence may yet throw a flood of light on the history of military operations and other topics of that eventful period, in which General and Senator Sherman were prominent figures.

He was among the first and most earnest advocates of the enlistment of colored men as soldiers.* Thus the soldiers have no truer friend than Senator Sherman, and but few with equal ability and influence to render them effective service.

SHERMAN ACCEPTABLE TO THE FRIENDS OF PEACE.

For twenty years there has been in the United States an organization known as the National Arbitration League. It is a universal peace union. An interesting and able address by R. McMurdy, D.D., LL.D., before one of its conventions held at Mystic, Conn., in August, 1884, was published with the following caption: "For Friends, Tunkers, Mennonites, Zoar and other communities, Shakers, and United Brethren whose fundamental principle is that of Peace; for Christians, whose

---

pension bill. which was the application of the same principle of liberality and justice to the dependent soldiers of the Union army that was approved by him in respect to the Mexican soldiers."

See Sherman's speech at Mt. Gilead, O., August 28, 1885, in which he said:

' While the Mexican pension bill was pending in the last Congress, I . . . preferred . . the *general disability amendment, allowing pensions to all disabled soldiers* who have arrived at a certain age, *without regard to the cause of disability.* I am now prepared to, and will when the subject is again presented, vote to place all pensioners upon the same footing as those who received pensions under the law as it stood prior to July 1, 1880. . . The general sentiment of the surviving soldiers of the war is that no discrimination shall be made in applications filed after July 1, 1880, but that all pensions shall commence from the disability, and I will vote to allow all pensions to commence from the date of disability.''

* See speech on Militia Bill in Senate, July 1, 1862.

founder organized the Great Universal Peace Union; for Business, Commercial, and Laboring men deeply interested in Peace."

The address puts and answers the inquiry: "How shall war be attacked and destroyed? We answer by the methods common to America in all cases of wide-spread evils, by press and speech, by church action and condemnation, and by the injection of the subject of arbitration into the currents of political thought and action."

The Republican National Platform of 1884 declares that "the Republican party favors a policy which shall keep us from entangling alliances with foreign nations; . . a *policy* which seeks peace and trade with all powers."

A very large, respectable, and conscientious body of intelligent American citizens have made a special study of international arbitration of public controversies in the interest of peace and humanity. Mr. Sherman, to use his own language, "has always been in favor of every measure to *preserve peace among nations,* and favored the law for arbitration of controversies between American States."

On the 8th of February, 1886, he introduced a bill in the Senate "for the encouragement of closer commercial relationship, and in the interest of and *the perpetuation of peace between* the United States and the republics of Mexico and Central and South America and the Empire of Brazil." This bill, in a preamble, recites that the people of the United States "desire to maintain the most friendly relations with and to encourage the *maintenance of peace* by and between said several States and people," and that for these purposes, and " to encourage a closer and more reciprocal intimacy in trade and commerce," it is considered that a great system of railroads extending from the United States through those countries " can be constructed through the united efforts of the several governments, . . guided by the advice and experience and assisted by material aid from the commercial and railroad interests of the United States."

The bill then provides that "the President of the United States is authorized to invite all the governments . . to send duly-appointed delegates to meet in convention in Washington, . . to consider such questions . . and adopt such measures as may be considered the most practical to carry forward the construction of said road in the *interest of peace,* commerce, and mutual prosperity."

With the American policy there is little or no danger of war with the nations of the Eastern hemisphere. Our chief dangers are liable to grow out of trade relations with the nations specified in the bill if entioned. With far-seeing, broad, comprehensive statesmanship, this great measure looks to universal enduring peace, with its attendant blessings of commercial prosperity.

Mr. Sherman is in a position to deserve and to receive the cordial and earnest support as a candidate for the Presidency of the vast body of conscientious citizens to which reference has been made.

SHERMAN IN AID OF HUMANITY IN WAR.

In October, 1863, an International Conference was held at Geneva, Switzerland, attended by delegates representing sixteen nations. After a session of four days it made a call for the " International Convention of Geneva" of 1864, which, by representatives of the same governments, adopted the "Red-Cross Treaty" of nine articles. It provides for the neutrality and security of hospitals in war, thus giving protection to the charitable and humane who volunteer their services as well as to those appointed by law. It provides for the neutrality and safety of chaplains, surgeons, and nurses even in the conflict of battle, and for other humanitarian arrangements. It gives sanction and protection to such organizations as the "Christian Commission" and the "Sanitary Commission," whose benevolent agencies were so useful during our late civil war. It enables them to extend their benevolence to the wounded of contending armies on both sides. The United States became a party to this treaty during the administration of President Arthur, and Senator Sherman aided in securing this result in the interest of universal humanity.

The National Association of the Red Cross has been organized in the United States in aid of the objects of the treaty.*

Thus the friends of universal humanity have in Mr. Sherman all that they can ask or desire.

---

* Clara Barton is President. She is world-renowned as volunteer in her works of charity and humanity on battle-fields and in prisons during our civil war, and since in similar works on the Island of Crete and in the Franco-Prussian war.

VII.

THE VALUE OF EXPERIENCE — THE LONG PUBLIC SERVICE OF MR. SHERMAN.

VII. MR SHERMAN *is the leading and most popular candidate in this, that he has been longer in the public service, has larger experience in public affairs, and has rendered more valuable services than any other candidate.*

In private employments the value of experience is recognized. He is the most popular applicant for such service who can perform it best. The "sober second thought" of the people demands that the best equipped man for public office shall fill it. He who has rendered most and best public service has claims to office as a reward for merit. To deny the justice of this claim, or the obligations to recognize it, is to give effect to the fallacy that "Republics are ungrateful."

The value of experience in official positions should be no less recognized than in professional and private employments. This is especially so in the greatest of all offices—the Presidency. As the President is required to recommend measures to Congress, he should be *familiar with its legislation,* with the structure of the Government, the resources and topography of the whole country,* the practical administration of its great departments, and our relations to other nations. Untried men, or those of limited experience, do not furnish sufficient evidence of all the requisite qualities. There have been times when *military men,* having proper civil qualifications, should be selected. The present and near future require experience and ability in civil affairs. Mr. Sherman has larger and more varied experience than any other candidate.

He was elected to Congress *in a Democratic district* in October, 1854, 1856, 1858, and 1860, and served in the 34th, 35th, and 36th Congresses. In March, 1861, he was elected to the Senate, to which he was re-elected in 1866 and again in 1872, and resigned March 5, 1877, when he became

---

* See Sherman's speech at Cincinnati March 26 1887, an extract from which is given above in note, showing his full knowledge of the condition of every State and Territory.

Secretary of the Treasury under President Hayes, in which capacity he served to March 3, 1881 ; and having in the mean time been re-elected to the Senate, was again re-elected in 1886 for the term of six years, commencing March 4, 1887.   He was elected, December 7, 1885, President of the Senate, thus becoming Vice-president.   He resigned that office February 27, 1887, and yet remains a Senator.

Here is a *continuous service of* over *thirty-three years,* not in one line of duty only, but so varied as to familiarize this illustrious statesman with all the great departments of the Government in their relations to our own people and to all other nations.   This period of service covers greater questions, greater events, and more stupendous achievements than have been crowded into any equal period of the world's history.

In his *first* term in the House of Representatives, Mr. Sherman rendered services to human freedom, the magnitude of which has been stated.   At the close of his second term he "was recognized as the foremost man in the House of Representatives."*   And in the 36th Congress he came within a few votes of being elected Speaker; but having declined, he was "recognized as the leader," and so made Chairman of the Committee of Ways and Means—the most important committee of the House.   On all questions he has had no superior during his service in the Senate, and on questions relating to *currency, revenue, and public credit*—questions in which all the people are more deeply interested now than any other—he is without any superior in this or any nation in any age of the world.

His work thus far has stood and will "stand the test of human scrutiny, of talents, and of time."   If for any brief period he entertained an erroneous opinion, it was soon corrected, and his work proves that he has *never made a mistake* in his final conclusions, in the measures he has secured, or the policies he has carried into execution.   Is there any other living statesman of whom as much can be said?

---

* Ben: Perley Poore, than whom there is no better judge. (Life of Sherman, p. 15.)

VIII.

THE WOOL-GROWING AND WOOLEN MANUFACTURING INDUSTRIES—SHERMAN THEIR SPECIAL ADVOCATE—EXCITEMENT OVER THE PRESIDENT'S MESSAGE—THE QUESTIONS IN THE CAMPAIGN OF 1888.

VIII. MR. SHERMAN *is the leading and most popular candidate in this, that he will command the united support of all the Republican wool-growers, and draw large support from Democrats engaged in that industry.*

The census of 1880 shows in the United States 1,020,728 flocks of sheep, exclusive of those on public land ranches. It may be assumed that there are *one million voters* who are flock-owners—one twelfth of all the voters in the United States—a political power the Republican party will not ignore. They hold in their hands the fate of other industries. Of these, in States nearly evenly balanced between the Republican and Democratic parties, Indiana has 54,069, Virginia 32,498, West Virginia 30,909, California a large number, and many in other States. These voters are probably half Republicans, half Democrats. If a Republican candidate be nominated who has not been a *pronounced friend of the wool industry*, he may lose enough Republican voters to insure his defeat. If such a friend of the wool industry be nominated, he will consolidate the Republican vote, and draw largely from the Democratic wool-growers.

Mr. Sherman is more prominently recognized as the advocate and friend of protection to this industry than any other candidate. He has done and said more than any other in its favor. In every tariff act passed by the Democratic party a low and inadequate duty was placed upon wool, and as a consequence foreign wool was largely imported; this industry did not prosper. The first Republican tariff, in 1861, imposed a higher duty on wool. This was found inadequate. In 1866–67 the manufacturers of woolens and the wool-growers united in asking Congress to increase duties, and a satisfactory tariff on wool and

woolen goods was provided in the act of March 2, 1867. Under this
the industries of wool-growing and wool-manufacturing prospered;
imports diminished; our producers largely supplied our own wants.*

The credit due to Mr. Sherman in securing the passage of the wool
tariff of 1867, and the harmony of interest thereby promoted for wool-
growers and manufacturers, is fairly stated by Mr. John L. Hayes,
Secretary of the National Association of Wool Manufacturers, in a
pamphlet published in 1886, in which he says:

"We appreciate too highly the benefits of the tariff of 1867 to forget
that *we owe the consummation of that great measure* mainly to . .
Sherman, Wade, Bingham, Delano, Lawrence, Garfield, Stansbury [and
other members of the House], and . . not less estimable private
citizens, Montgomery and Stevens. Mr. Sherman, Chairman of the
Senate Finance Committee, on the last day but one of the second
session of the 39th Congress, carried the . . bill now known as 'the
tariff of 1867' through his committee and finally through the Senate."

Thus Mr. Sherman was conspicuous in giving to the wool-growers
the first great tariff act to secure the permanence and prosperity of
their industry. Without his efforts the law never would have been
passed. Surely he may now be justly called the wool-growers' and
wool-manufacturers' candidate; and as a matter of self-interest, of duty,
and of justice on their part, he is entitled to their support.

In 1881 the revenues from tariff and internal taxes became largely
in excess of the wants of the Government, and a commission· was
appointed to report a revision. On the 5th of August, 1882, Senator
Bayard, a Democrat, offered an amendment to a bill to reduce the duty
on wool to twenty-five per cent *ad valorem*, equal to about four cents a
pound specific duty on clothing and combing wools. This was voted for
by Democrats and defeated by Republicans.†

The Tariff Commission made their report to Congress December 4,
1882, and a bill based thereon proposed to repeal most of the then
existing internal revenue taxes, and to reduce some tariff duties, including those on wool.‡ The President of the National Wool-growers'

---

* No. 42 Statement Bureau of Statistics on Wool, September 10, 1884; Report No. 37,
January and February, 1887, Agricultural Department; Quarterly Report Bureau of Statistics, March 31, 1885.

† Congressional Record, Vol. XIV., Part III., p. 2144.

‡ The duty under act of 1867: *Clothing* wool, thirty-two cents or less, ten cents per pound
and eleven per cent *ad valorem*; over thirty-two cents, twelve cents per pound and eleven per
cent *ad valorem*; washed, twice these duties; *Combing* wool, thirty-two cents or less, ten cents
per pound and eleven per cent *ad valorem*; over thirty-two cents, twelve cents per pound and
ten per cent *ad valorem*; *Carpet* wool, twelve cents or less, three cents; and over twelve cents,

Association, Mr. Garland, of Illinois, assented to this reduction.* Mr. Sherman *opposed the reduction*, but he was defeated. He offered an amendment to increase the duty to twelve and fourteen cents per pound, which was *then satisfactory to wool-growers*; but his amendment was defeated; a majority of the Republicans voting for it, the Democrats, with three exceptions and a few others, against it. The bill in most though not in all other respects was desirable. It embraced a great number of articles, and reduced taxation $60,000,000 annually. It removed all internal revenue taxes except those on whisky, tobacco, and beer. Of course Mr. Sherman could not vote against it. Its effect upon the wool industry has been injurious, if not disastrous. Under it imports of wool have increased; the number of sheep in the United States has diminished.‡

In 1883, before the reduction, the wool clip of the country was 350,000,000 pounds; average value thirty cents, or $105,000,000; in 1887 the clip was only 260,000,000 pounds; average value twenty cents, or $52,000,000; a loss to the wool-growers of $53,000,000. We *import* now more wool on the scoured basis than we raise, including wool in the form of manufactured goods. One third of the woolen and worsted goods we consume is imported.

Recent events have given new and great importance to the question of protection to the American wool industry and to the manufacturers of woolen and worsted goods. These industries go together. "United they stand, divided they fall."

The Democratic Secretary of the Treasury, in his report of December 6, 1886, says:

"I respectfully recommend to Congress . . the immediate passage of an act simply and solely placing raw wool upon the free list. Of course, a repeal of the duty on raw wool should be followed by . .

---

six cents per pound. All classes scoured, treble duty. The act of March 3, 1883: *Clothing* wool, value thirty cents or less, ten cents per pound; over thirty cents, twelve cents per pound; washed, twice these rates; *Combing* wool, value thirty cents or less, ten cents per pound; over thirty cents, twelve cents per pound; *Carpet* wool, value twelve cents or less, two and one half cents per pound; over twelve cents, five cents per pound. Treble duties on all scoured wools.

* Sherman's speech at Ohio State Fair, Columbus, September 1, 1887.

† Congressional Record, Vol. XIV., Part III., pp. 2144, 2965-2974; Sherman's speech at Washington, O., September 13, 1883, Cincinnati Commercial Gazette, September 15, 1883; Toledo speech, Toledo Blade, September 21, 1883; speech at Portsmouth, O., September 28, 1886, in which he says, "I earnestly and heartily opposed the reduction"

‡ Report No. 37 on Farm Animals. Department of Agriculture, January and February, 1887, p. 35; New York Tariff League Bulletin, November, 1887.

a compensating adjustment [reduction] of the .duties on manufactured woolens."

And the President, in his message of December 6, 1887, substantially concurs in the recommendation by saying: "The farmer . . is told that a high duty on imported wool is necessary for the benefit of those who have sheep to shear." The President then proceeds with what he calls "reasons," and says they "are suggested why the *removal* or reduction of this duty should be included in a revision of our tariff laws."

The removal or a reduction of the wool tariff *will work the destruction of our wool industry*, and with it will perish the manufacture of woolen and worsted goods. The present tariff on wool and on worsted goods is inadequate; the numbers of our sheep are fast decreasing when they should be increasing.

In the face of this threatened destruction of these important industries great alarm has been excited throughout the whole country. Even prior to this the necessity for an *increase* of the wool tariff was urgently demanded. The Farmers' National Congress at Indianapolis, in 1885, demanded "a restoration of the wool tariff of 1867;" a like demand was made by the similar congress at St. Paul, in August, 1886; and the similar congress at Chicago, in November, 1887, demanded a *progressively increasing* tariff on wool until it shall give the American wool-growers the exclusive privilege of supplying all the wool required by American wants. A substantially similar demand was made on behalf of American manufacturers.

Mr. Sherman has never faltered in his devotion to these interests. Soon after the reduced wool tariff of 1883, in a speech at Toledo, September 20, 1883, he said:

"In all the Democratic tariffs . . no duty on wool was ever fixed higher than five cents per pound. . . In 1867 the wool-growers and wool-manufacturers met together; . . and then the Republican party . . in 1867 passed a law which gave us a duty on certain grades, worth thirty-two cents or less, of ten cents per pound and eleven per cent *ad valorem;* and on wool which was worth more it was twelve cents per pound and eleven per cent *ad valorem.* This tariff, which gave satisfactory protection to growers of wool, was voted for by every Republican in Congress. . . It was voted against by every Democrat in Congress. In 1881 it was proposed by Mr. Bayard, an old member of the Democratic party, to *put the duty down* to twenty-five per cent *ad valorem.* As the average foreign valuation is about sixteen cents a pound, the proposed duty was something like four or five cents a pound. All the Democrats . . voted for that proposition."

He then refers to the tariff bill of 1883 and its consideration in the Senate, and says:

"I offered an amendment in the Senate to restore the duty on wool to twelve and fourteen cents on different grades. That proposition was supported by me and other Republicans in debate. When the vote came upon it, every Democrat but three voted against it. . . It was the Democratic party that lowered the tariff on wool; . . but they say we Republicans are responsible because, although the *Democrats prevented the restoration* of the tariff on wool [the Sherman amendment], we voted for the tariff bill. It was a bill that embraced more than a thousand different articles. It lifted off the shoulders of the people of the United States $77,000,000 of taxes [annually]. . . It took off all internal [revenue] taxes, except upon whisky, tobacco, and beer, and it left ample protective duties on most of the industries."

In a speech at Columbus, September 24, 1884, referring to the tariff act of March 3, 1883, he said:

"In dealing with the tariff, however, sufficient care was not taken to maintain or extend the *principle of protection of the then existing law* on the great article of wool produced by a million farmers; . . and the duty on the **raw forms of iron**—such as pig iron, scrap iron, and iron ore— was also unwisely reduced. I have always thought, and still think, that this was a grave error. This blunder . . was committed by the Democratic party, with the aid of a few Republicans."

And he then proceeds to show that when an attempt was made by Hon. George L. Converse, in the House of Representatives, to secure the consideration of a bill to restore the duty on wool, "he was met by jeers and laughter" by the Democratic members of that body, and his proposition was defeated by a vote of 126 nays to 119 yeas.*

In the demand for increased protection the wool-growers are in earnest. A National Convention of Wool-growers, held at St. Louis, May 13, 1887, resolved that "this convention requests Congress to so amend the existing tariff law as in due time to secure to American wool-growers and to American manufacturers of woolens the American market for their products." At a meeting of the Ohio wool-growers at Columbus, September 1, 1887, it was resolved "that we concur in all the resolutions passed at the late convention in St. Louis."

Mr. Sherman was then called on to address the wool-growers, and, among other things, said:

"When you . . say that the present tariff has injured your production of wool, and has diminished the number of sheep produced in this country, you make a complaint that *ought to be remedied*, and I assure you that if

---

* See Congressional Record, Vol. XV., pages 3733–8.

one Senator can do any thing to bring you substantially back to your position in 1867, *I will try to do it.*"

And he referred to the fact that, "under a new process," foreign scoured clothing and combing wool is imported under the name of "waste," under a ruling of the Treasury Department, at a low rate of duty. Under Sherman's administration of the Treasury Department no such evasion was permitted.*

The Ohio State Grange, at its session at Canton, December 15, 1887, resolved "against any further reduction in the tariff on wool," and demanded "the restoration of the wool tariff of 1867."

The wool-growers, wool-dealers, and wool-manufacturers are so thoroughly aroused that committees representing the two former classes met in Washington City December 5, 1887, and after a session lasting several days they published an address, in which they say :

"The wool-dealers and wool-growers of the United States, representing a capital of over $500,000,000 and a constituency of a million of wool-growers and wool-dealers, . . declare that the sentiments of the [President's recent] message are a direct attack upon our industry, one of the most important of the country, and in positive violation of the National Democratic Platform of 1884, as interpreted by the party leaders and accepted by the rank and file of the party. . . Justly alarmed at his position, we make an appeal from his recommendations to the people—to all the people—to the seven and three fourths millions of our fellow-citizens engaged in agriculture—to the millions engaged in manufacturing—to the army of wage-earners, whose wages are maintained by the protective system—to the tradesmen and merchants whose prosperity depends upon ours—confident that their judgment and decision will be based upon justice and patriotism, and therefore for the maintenance of the American policy of protection, to which the country is indebted for its unexampled development. The annual revenue derived from imports of wool under the tariff of 1867 was less than $1,700,000. Under the reduced tariff of 1883 the revenue last year was over $5,000,000. The

---

* Justice, Bateman & Co., of Philadelphia, in their wool circular of December 15, 1887, say:

"The past week has been most eventful in the history of the wool trade. Two events of startling surprise and momentous importance have occurred. The first is the attack of the President of the United States upon the wool interests in his message to Congress; the second is the decision on the 7th inst. of the United States Court of this District to the effect that such articles of carded and combed scoured wool as are known under various names, but classified as wastes, are not dutiable at thirty cents per pound as scoured wool, according to previous customs rulings, but at ten cents per pound as waste. This wipes out a large measure of the protection which the present tariff was intended to afford to wool-growing."

The wool-growers have suffered by fraudulent undervaluations on imported wool. On the 21st of January, 1884, the Senate passed a resolution, introduced by Mr. Sherman, requiring a report by the Secretary of the Treasury on that subject. With him as President these frauds would not be permitted, but all fairly doubtful questions would be resolved in favor of American wool-growers and manufacturers.

number of sheep in the country in 1884 was 50,626,626; in 1887, 44,759,314, a decrease of nearly 6,000,000, and a diminution of the annual wool product of over 35,000,000 pounds; thus showing that reducing the tariff by the act of 1883 has increased the revenue of imported wool and diminished the number of sheep in the United States about twelve per cent, and the annual product in the same proportion. The President's policy would bring about the destruction of this industry, and the same policy of reduction or abolition of the tariff would end in disaster to all the other industrial productive enterprises of the country."

And arrangements have been perfected for a joint meeting in Washington, commencing January 11, 1888, of committees representing the wool-growers, wool-dealers, and manufacturers of woolen and worsted goods, to carry on the work of appealing to the American people.*

It is to be observed that the Farmers' National Congress, the Ohio State Grange, the Ohio Wool-growers' Association, and the St. Louis Wool-growers' National Convention were, and the committees above-mentioned are, composed alike of Democrats and Republicans, earnestly determined to be heard by Congress and in the presidential contest of 1888.

Mr. Cleveland will undoubtedly be the Democratic candidate for the Presidency in 1888. He will hear from a million of wool-growers and hundreds of thousands of manufacturers in the political contest of that year. Who so eminently fit to meet him in that contest as Mr. Sherman? Who can so fully command the votes of the wool-growers and manufacturers as he? Necessarily the effect of his prominence as the advocate of such protection as will give the whole American market to American wool-growers and American woolen and worsted manufacturers is that he will take the entire Republican vote and a large share of those who are Democrats interested in these industries. The wool-growers in several doubtful States can turn the scale in favor of Sherman and secure his election if nominated.

---

* Since the foregoing was written a convention of the committee above named was held, which after a session of four days, ending January 14th, presented the draft of a tariff bill agreed upon for wool and woolen and worsted goods.

IX.

CIVIL-SERVICE REFORM—MR. SHERMAN A PIONEER IN ITS FAVOR—HE IS ACCEPTABLE TO CIVIL-SERVICE REFORMERS.

IX. MR. SHERMAN *is an available candidate in this, that he will command the confidence and support of the friends of " Civil-service Reform."*

In the presidential election of 1884 there was a class of Republicans, especially in New York, known as "Civil-service Reformers"—sometimes called "Mugwumps"—led by George William Curtis, Carl Schurz, and Henry Ward Beecher. They opposed "personal government" and strong "personality" in the appointing power. They supported the Democratic candidate, Mr. Cleveland, and *took from the Republican party enough votes to turn New York against it.* New York may decide the next contest, and Republican success requires a candidate who can solidify the Republicans of that State. Mr. Sherman is acceptable generally to Civil-service Reformers, and can carry New York.

The leading purpose of the Civil-service Reformers is to remove the "spoils system" from non-political appointments. When the Government started under Washington it was administered on the principle that men should be appointed to office for merit, not partisanship. Washington kept in his Cabinet Jefferson, who was hostile to his administration. Jefferson, to secure his election by Congress as President, reluctantly wrote a letter promising that in appointments the only question should be, "Is he honest, capable, and faithful to the constitution?" After he was elected he was restive under his pledge, and in reference to Federalists in office regretted that "few die and none resign." In a limited way he broke his pledge, but the original policy prevailed until 1832, when a Democrat, Mr. Marcy, proclaimed that

" to the victors belong the spoils."*   Although President Jackson had previously written a letter against the "spoils system," he yielded to pressure, and removed nearly all office-holders politically opposed to him, and appointed his partisans in their places.

When Mr. Lincoln became President, it became necessary to make general changes to secure loyal men in office.   President Grant recommended to Congress a reform in the civil service, and Congress passed a law to effect that object, for which Mr. Sherman voted.†   Mr. Curtis was Chairman of the Commission under that act.   President Hayes went still further by making removals only for cause, and enjoining on office-holders non-interference with elections when prejudicial to the public service.‡   Mr. Sherman, Secretary of the Treasury under President Hayes, faithfully carried out the principles of civil-service reform.§

As early as January 26, 1869, he reported back to the Senate a bill reorganizing the Treasury Department, and offered a concurrent resolution, finally agreed to by the House March 2, 1869, providing for a joint committee " to examine and report upon the expediency of reorganizing the civil service in the several departments, and for " a more economical and efficient performance of the civil service."|| It will thus be seen he, in some measure, is a *pioneer* in this work.   On January 4, 1871, he spoke in favor of Trumbull's bill to prohibit members of Congress from interfering in appointments to office.¶

The National Republican Platform of 1872 declared that " any system of civil service under which the subordinate [non-political] positions of the Government are considered rewards for mere party zeal is fatally demoralizing, and we therefore demand a reform of the system which shall abolish the evils of patronage, and make honesty, efficiency, and fidelity essential qualifications for public positions without creating a life-tenure of office."

Congress finally passed the " Pendleton " civil-service act of January 16, 1883.   It has been practically ignored or evaded by Cleveland's administration.   Mr. Sherman favored the principles and purposes of this

---

* Blaine, Vol. II., p. 644.

† Act of March 3, 1871.

‡ Inaugural Address, Cong. Record, Vol. VI., Appendix, p. 3; Annual Message December 3, 1877, Cong. Record, Vol. VII., Part I , p. 3; Message December 1, 1879, Cong. Record, Vol. X., Part I., p. 3; Message December 2, 1880, Cong. Record. Vol. XI., Part I., p. 2; see President's Circular in 4 Lawrence Comptroller's Decisions, p 488.

§ Bronson's Life of Sherman, p. 234.

|| Cong. Globe and Appendix, 1st Session 41st Congress, 1869, p. 45.

¶ See speech January 4, 1871, Cong. Globe, Part I., 3d session 41st Congress, p. 293; Cong. Globe, Part I., 2d Session, 41st Congress, p. 17.

measure.* As President he would faithfully carry out its provisions. He has not encountered the antagonism of Civil-service Reformers; *their opposition never has been aimed at him. His nomination would secure a vote which will insure success in New York.*

X.

THE SILVER MINING INDUSTRY—SHERMAN THE FRIEND OF THIS INDUSTRY—ITS NEEDS—CHINESE LABORERS —SHERMAN FAVORS THEIR EXCLUSION.

X. MR. SHERMAN *is an available candidate in this, that he will command the solid support of the Republicans of the Pacific Coast and the mining regions.*

The people of California, Oregon, and Nevada are generally opposed to the admission of Chinese laborers. When the Chinese first began to immigrate, and for some time thereafter, no opposition was made. For some purposes their coming was encouraged. The people as yet had not foreseen the injury to the labor of American citizens and the danger to our institutions. It is not strange that some eminent statesmen, fearing the effect of violating treaty stipulations with China, did not at first approve measures in Congress to restrict Chinese immigration.†

Mr. Sherman is earnestly opposed to such immigration, and voted for the act of July 5, 1884, to prevent it,‡ and subsequently as Chairman of the Committee on Foreign Affairs reported back another bill with amendments to secure the same object § On this subject his position meets the approval of all opposed to such immigration.

Nevada and other States are largely interested in silver mining. The demonetization of silver, or a limitation in amount as to the legal-tender

----

* Cong. Record, Vol. XIV., Part I., pp. 209–247, 361, 640, 648, 661.

† Congressional Record, Vol. XIII., pp. 1747–1751, 2606–2615; Arthur's veto, April 14, 1882, p. 2571. Act of Congress May 6, 1882, called "Chinese Bill."

‡ Congressional Record, Vol. XV., p. 5938.

§ Senate proceedings, April 29 and May 6, 1880, Cong. Record, Vol. XVII., pp. 4958–4962, 5100.

quality of silver coin, would impair the value of silver mines and be prejudicial to the mining industry. The debtor class would suffer by it, because it would enhance gold, the only remaining coin with which to pay debts. The same interests which require bi-metallic money here insist on treaty arrangements with other nations to preserve it there. Demonetization in Europe would destroy the foreign demand for silver coin, for which our people want a market as they do for other products. Mr. Sherman has always been in favor of silver coinage,* and of preserving unimpaired its legal-tender quality, and *he incorporated this in his Resumption Act of January* 14, 1875. He made a speech in the Senate in favor of investigating the complaint that the Assistant Treasurer at New Orleans declined to receive silver dollars and issue certificates therefor as required by law. He favored silver coin with sufficient metal therein to make their commercial value equal to gold coins of the same denomination.† He has favored the several " International Monetary Conferences" with foreign nations to secure silver coinage, and on the 9th of December, 1867, introduced a resolution into the Senate directing the Secretary of State to furnish the correspondence in respect to the International Monetary Conference held in France June and July, 1867.

England is one of the nations which limits the legal-tender capacity of silver to forty shillings. The result is, our silver coins as such will not buy products in that country. With a view to secure an international ratio, Mr. Sherman, on the 7th of January, 1876, introduced a resolution into the Senate, adopted June 7th, "proposing a convention to secure uniformity in coins and money between the United States and Great Britain."

Thus, on these great questions, Mr. Sherman has been and is *fully alive to American interests,* and as President he can be relied on for vigorous and effectual service in their behalf.

---

* See speech in Senate, June 8, 1876.

† Congressional Record, Vol. XVII., pp 7463-7465; same volume, p. 942; Senator Eustis's resolution in Senate, February 8, 1886; speech at Portsmouth, O., September 28, 1886; Sherman's speech in San Francisco, in 1886, was entirely satisfactory to those in the silver industry.

XI.

GENERAL REPUBLICAN POLICY — ITS MANY GREAT MEASURES — SHERMAN THE ADVOCATE OF ALL — SECURITY FOR RIGHTS OF NATURALIZED CITIZENS — THE HOMESTEAD LAWS — RESERVE THE PUBLIC LANDS FOR ACTUAL SETTLERS — GERMAN VOTERS— IRISH VOTERS.

XI. MR. SHERMAN *is an available candidate in this, that he has been and is the earnest, efficient advocate of all the great measures and purposes of the Republican party.*

Reference has already been made to some of these. It is not possible to enumerate all.

Mr. Sherman gave his support to legislation declaring that "all naturalized citizens . . while in foreign countries . . shall receive protection,"* thus asserting the right of *expatriation*—a right further protected by numerous treaties which he aided to ratify. His liberal, enlightened opinions have drawn to him the confidence of Germans and other naturalized citizens, so much so that it was with difficulty he could resist the wish of leading citizens of Ohio, in 1883, to leave his place in the Senate to lead the Republican party to victory as a candidate for Governor. His *great popularity* was conceded on all hands, and it is further proved by the results of every election in Ohio in which his candidacy was involved as Senator from Ohio and when a candidate for Representative in Congress, as already stated. His position is equally satisfactory to the Irish-American citizens. No man has been or is more pronounced as the friend of the Irish in Ireland than he. It was in view of this that he was invited to preside over the meeting held in Washington City December 14, 1887, in honor of Hon. Arthur O'Connor and Sir Thomas Henry Grattan Esmonde's visit to Washington, and to

---

* Act of July 27, 1868, Rev. Stat. 2000.

express American sympathy for Ireland. On that occasion he delivered an address, and among other things said:

"I can assure your distinguished guests to-hight that there is a general and hearty sympathy in all parts of our country and with all classes of our people with the movement now pending to secure to the people of Ireland home rule, or the management of all their local affairs to the full extent demanded by Mr. Parnell and Mr. Gladstone. This is not merely because they are Irishmen, but because they are free men. The same sympathy would be extended to any people seeking the same rights. It is a doctrine of American policy that the power of government should emanate as directly as possible from the people, and be distributed from all their political organizations—from the head of the family, the school district, the township, the county, the State, and the nation. We believe that this policy of local home rule and the diversity of agents is the only one by which it is possible to unite people of different ideas, productions, occupations, and localities into a great and powerful free nation.   .   .   .   .   .

"It is natural that when any portion of the people of the mother country, from whence the great body of our population sprang, demand home rule for themselves in matters affecting their local interests as distinguished from the general powers of the empire, for every American, proud of his form of government, to wish for our kindred across the sea the same rights that we enjoy. When, therefore, Mr. Gladstone, the greatest living statesman of his country and perhaps of the world, saw a mode by which these rights can be conferred upon the people of Ireland, who have complained for generations of woes unnumbered and wrongs unredressed, we naturally hoped that the British Parliament would yield to their demands. This claim was also pressed with modesty but firmness by Mr. Parnell as the leader of the Irish people. I met him here on his visit some years ago, and was impressed with the moderation of his demand. He seemed to have the earnest enthusiasm of the . Irishman, the caution of the Scotchman, and the tenacity of the Englishman, and I sincerely hoped for him, as I do still, that he might persuade the British Parliament to yield a local autonomy to Ireland that would enable her people through their own legislature to make laws for their own people in respect to all matters not involving imperial authority, or what we would call the union of the empire.

"I believe that home rule in Ireland would be a blessing to England as well. From the standpoint of our example the Imperial Parliament of Great Britain ought not to be occupied with local laws for any portion of that great empire. This principle has been of late years applied so that now nearly all the colonies of Great Britain have each a separate autonomy with a local legislature of even more extensive powers than are reserved to the States under our form of government. Our neighbor, the Dominion of Canada, has complete power over its local affairs, and yet it is composed of a mixed population, including many savage tribes of Indians and vast, unoccupied regions.

"Ireland, on the other hand, is a populous region that has con-
tributed its full part to all the grandeur of the British Empire.   Its
soldiers have carried the flag of that country in the front of every battle
in which the British army has been engaged in modern times   Its poets
have made not only their love-songs, but their national anthems.   Its
orators are quoted throughout the world as the most eminent in history.
The name of Henry Grattan will be remembered forever not only for
his eloquence, but for his patriotism.   The wonderful vigor of its population, its productions, its history, and its literature bear evidence of the
fitness for the highest duties that can rest upon a people.

"Surely under the circumstances it would seem but a slight boon to
give them the same local power and privileges they enjoyed for generations, and the same authority over home affairs as has been conferred
upon the far distant province of Canada; and this, as I understand, is all
they ask.   The union, strength, and power of the British Empire will
not be weakened by the gift of home rule to Ireland, and the delay in
granting this great act of justice will only continue the animosities of
the past, and add to the alienation between races of men who are bound
together by proximity of situation and by historic ties.

"I believe that your guests can carry back to their country the
assurance that while our sympathy may be of no service to them in their
struggle, yet so far as it will encourage them they have it in the hearts
and in the hopes of the great body of our countrymen."

Mr. Sherman's name is a power; he *has never been defeated for any
office for which he has been nominated.*   He has been the earnest friend of
the *homestead policy,* and will receive cordial support of the hardy
pioneers who have secured homes thereby—more than half a million in
number.   While favoring the policy of land-grant aid to railroad com-
panies in new States *at the time when most needed,* and conservative of all
vested rights, yet he has " voted for the repeal of every grant where there
has not been a substantial compliance, or an active and reasonable effort
to comply with the grant," * and he has long since favored the policy of
making no further grants, but of *reserving the lands for actual settlers,* and
of forbidding sales for speculation.

He has been the efficient advocate of internal improvement to secure
cheap transportation on all the great waterways of the country.†   He has
maintained that Congress should *regulate railroad and water transportation*
of interstate commerce, to secure the same great object.‡

There is *not one question* on which his opinions are not known and
accessible, and on them all he is right.   With such a candidate for the
Presidency in 1888, success will be certain.

---

* Speech at Wilmington, Ohio, September 15, 1887.

† Nashville speech, March 21, 1887.

‡ Portsmouth (Ohio) speech, September 23, 1886.

XII.

THE AGRICULTURISTS — THEIR INDUSTRIES SAFE IN SHERMAN'S HANDS — THE SUGAR INDUSTRY — THE SORGHUM SUGAR INDUSTRIES OF KANSAS.

XII. MR. SHERMAN *is the leading and most popular candidate in this, that he can command more votes of the agriculturists than any other.*

His claims upon wool-growers have been considered. The farmers know that more than ninety per cent of all their products are consumed by the *home market*, which is largely created by industries dependent upon protective duties for their existence and continuance.* No statesman excels Mr. Sherman in zeal or ability in securing and continuing protective duties. He has supported all the measures ever devised in Congress for the advancement of agricultural interests, including the creation of the Department of Agriculture. He was the *first* to ask the Senate to add to the committees of that body a Committee on Agriculture, as he successfully did by a resolution for that purpose March 6, 1863, and he was made chairman of the committee.

One subject requires early and careful consideration. The Republican doctrine is that those industries should be protected which by protection can be sufficiently developed to supply the wants of our people. Such protection does not ultimately enhance the cost to the consumer, because home competition has always secured products cheaper than imports.

Protective duties on raw sugar have thus far failed to develop the cane-sugar industry sufficiently to supply our wants, and the result is that the duty on sugar as yet is a *tax on the consumer*. The value of sugar and molasses imported in the fiscal year 1886 was $76,723,266; the duty collected thereon, $51,766,923. Our annual consumption of foreign and domestic sugar is about forty pounds per head of population. Thus we

---

* See Sherman's Nashville speech, March 21, 1887, in which he says:

" We give to the farmer a home market for home productions, so that now of all the products of the farm over ninety per cent is consumed in this country and less than ten per cent exported abroad, though the aggregate of exportations of food products amount to nearly $500,000,000."

are paying large sums of money to other countries for sugar, and they especially buy but little of our products. If the present duty on sugar be continued, without an early increase of our sugar product, it will be an oppressive tax on consumers, and yet it would be unjust to the Louisiana, Texas, and Florida planters, who have invested money on the faith of protection,' to abandon them to destruction. Free trade in sugar, with *no inducement to increase our sugar product*, would prevent the further development of cane sugar and destroy the prospect of developing the product of sorghum sugar, beet sugar, and glucose from corn. Recent experiments in the new "diffusion of saturation process" of extracting saccharine from sorghum, conducted at Fort Scott, Kansas, by Mr. Colman, the able and efficient Commissioner of Agriculture, show that ninety-eight per cent of saccharine can now be extracted from sorghum and sugar-cane, whereas by old methods seventy per cent at most could be secured. As to this industry Mr. Sherman has said:

"There should be a decided reduction in the tariff on sugar, and then a bounty should be paid on American sugar sufficiently generous to procure *the production of all the sugar in the United States that our people may consume*. We have the best soil in the world for the sugar-beet and the sorghum-cane, covering almost limitless acres. We ought to produce all the sugar we consume, and we may reasonably do so by a *judicious tariff* and *liberal bounties* to producers. . . It is the same as it was in regard to iron and steel and other products. We used to think we had to depend upon foreign countries for these."*

Commissioner Coleman recently said of sorghum-sugar production:

"There is an overproduction of most farm products, making prices ruinously low; and if this new industry will employ a portion of those now raising other things at no profit, it will give great relief to the farming classes and open a most promising field for both farmer and manufacturer. . . At the end of the next twenty-five years we will be paying at least $200,000,000 for sugar per year. This money we can keep at home and distribute among our people."

In a brief speech at the Ohio State Fair at Columbus, September 1, 1887, Mr. Sherman said:

"There is one lesson of many lessons we can learn from the oldest

---

* Interview in Cincinnati Enquirer of June 16, 1887: see Sherman's speech, Springfield, Ill., June 1, 1887, in which he said:

"A protective duty has been placed on sugar for the benefit of the sugar-planters of Louisiana, but we now propose, as one means of reducing surplus revenue, to largely reduce this tax, and as a protection to sugar-growers some propose to pay out of the duties on sugar a bounty for the home production of all kinds of sugar from cane or beets or sorghum. This policy of protection has been extended to the products of the farm, the yield of the mines, as well as the fabrics of the mechanic and the manufacturer. In this way the levying of taxes is made the means of national growth and development, nearly trebling in twenty years our domestic manufactures, and at the same time by competition reducing the prices."

nations of Europe. With large cities growing up around us the farmer becomes a gardener. The lesser crops yield the greater profit. In Germany, France, and Italy they are now raising more sugar from beets than is produced in all the world from sugar-cane. The people of the United States now pay $130,000,000 for sugar which can easily be produced from beets grown in any of the Central States. We must in Ohio keep up with the most advanced of our sister States. If we are pressed with competition and discouraged by drought and low prices, we must remember, after all, that other communities have their drawbacks, and that we have our advantages and privileges that make us one of the most, if not the most, favored community in the world."

And the report adds that "Mr. Sherman at considerable length stated the growth of the beet-sugar industry as developed in France and Germany, and of the capacity of the United States to supply the home demand."

The State of Kansas recently provided by law for the payment of two cents per pound bounty for all sorghum sugar produced in that State. The indications are that Kansas and other States will, in the near future, vastly increase the sugar product. The policy of national aid to a great struggling industry for existence, growth, and development has found favor in many nations.

It is certainly better to pay for a limited time bounties from an overflowing treasury to our *own people*, and thereby secure our supply from our sugar-cane, sorghum, and sugar-beets, and thus relieve farmers from the depression of their present industries, rather than pay immense sums annually to foreigners. It will not cost the people so much as it does to pay the duties of which it is proposed to relieve them.* Every farmer and every citizen of the United States is interested in the policy proposed by Mr. Sherman—a policy pursued in other nations, but thus far neglected by our own, except as the State of Kansas has inaugurated the policy of bounties for the production of sorghum sugar. This policy properly pursued would add to the value of every farm, to the value of all products, and to the benefit of the whole country. The producers of

---

* Mr. Sherman, in his speech in the Senate January 4, 1888, said of articles imported during the last fiscal year:

"The articles of sugar, fruit, and rice, valued at $90,898,000, paid a duty of $63,190.000. . . These are articles which enter into the consumption of every family. Now, if the object is to reduce surplus revenue, what better mode could be suggested than to repeal one half of the duty on sugar, and thus directly relieve the people of $28,250,000 of taxes on an article in most general use by the people, . . and bearing a tax of eighty-two per cent."

If a bounty of one cent a pound should be paid on all the sugar produced in the United States, it would amount annually to about $2,317,990. Thus a reduction of the tariff tax of one half would save the people from a burden of $28,250,000, and the bounty would cost them only one tenth of this sum.

sugar would realize the advantages of a bounty directly paid to them in money more readily than those of high duties. The bounties would more speedily and fully develop the industry. But if these can not be adequately secured by National and State aid, a sufficiently protective tariff must be maintained while there is a reasonable prospect of thereby developing the sugar industry sufficiently to supply American wants.

Mr. Sherman is emphatically the candidate of the American farmers, a class of intelligent voters, comprising fifty-four per cent of all, and whose industry is the basis of all others.

The people will properly ask as to every candidate, What has he done for the public good? What measures has he originated? The answer as to Mr. Sherman can be readily made. Let the question be asked as to all candidates.

The nomination of Mr. Sherman will insure success and restore the Government to the party which has a grander record than any that ever lived since the Declaration of Independence.

Thus *some*—and *only* some—of the prominent events in the life of Mr. Sherman have been given; so *some*—and *only* some—of the prominent reasons have been presented which render his nomination as the Republican candidate for the Presidency in 1888 eminently "wise and judicious."

CONCLUSION.*

The life of John Sherman represents the growth and the capacities of man under the free institutions of this Republic. From the school-room to the court-house, the Capitol, and the Treasury Department, he has done his duty with ability and with fidelity. Self-reliant, he has risen by the firmness of his character and the brilliancy of his intellect to the high position first graced by Hamilton. An accomplished scholar, a learned lawyer, a fearless and enlightened legislator, a far-seeing and upright member of the Cabinet, an honorable gentleman in private life, and a confiding friend, he has ever been noted for his comprehensive intellect, his conscientious integrity, and his adherence to those conservative and constitutional principles of government which secure to every citizen his rights, and to every section its equal consideration

---

* The "conclusion" above given is from Ben: Perley Poore's "Life and Public Services of John Sherman," written in 1880, but is equally true and applicable now

under the administration of just laws. The dark corruptions of the war epoch have never clouded his reputation, nor has any tongue ever ventured to impeach his honor, for his life has been pure and unsullied, while it has been brilliant and useful.

Mr. Sherman is now in the prime of manhood—tall, firmly built, yet graceful in his movements, and capable of great endurance. His features are expressive, and there is a good-humored twinkle in his bluish-gray eyes, while his forehead and the lower portion of his face indicate positive determination and adherence. His style of oratory is colloquial and convincing, a vein of practical common sense running through its series of arguments until a convincing conclusion is reached. The rapidity with which he takes up the strong points of a case and successively disposes of them renders him a formidable adversary in debate. Careful not to infringe upon the rights or to wound the feelings of others, he demands in return from others perfect respect towards himself.

The National Republican Convention which is to meet at Chicago in June should nominate for President of the United States a man capable of surveying the whole field connected with the interests of the country, who can furnish Congress with the information called for by the Constitution, and can make such recommendations as will be of practical value in shaping legislation—a man of the people, who has been the architect of his own fortunes, upon whose public and personal record there rests no stain—a man who has been tested by honorably filling high positions, and who is thoroughly acquainted with our machinery of government—a man whose life, whose principles, whose speeches, and whose character are filled with humanity—a man whose nomination must strengthen and consolidate the Republican party. If the convention seeks such a man, let it nominate one whose name is familiar to every intelligent citizen of the Union as having maintained its credit in dark hours and successfully restored specie payments. Let them nominate John Sherman, of Ohio.

The nomination of Mr. Sherman in June will result in his triumphant election by the voters of the United States in November. His patriotism, his ability, his private virtues, and his public services will command him the hearty support of every true Republican, of every friend of good administration, of every lover of honest money. With him as a candidate, the Republican party can receive no assault which can dim the glory of the past or impede the progress of the future. His triumph will be the triumph of union and liberty, of the rights of the people, of the prosperity and the glory of the Republic.

With John Sherman as President, the United States would have a Government whose intercourse with other nations would be marked with that high degree of international justice which would neither do nor tolerate wrong; a Government which would be administered at home by sound and pure men, who would regard offices as solemn trusts and not as partisan spoils; a Government marked by a lofty tone of public morality, mild yet efficient, conservative yet liberal; a Government which would maintain the rights of the humblest citizens, and would seek the advancement of American industry and the extension of American markets; a Government under which Republican principles would be predominant through the length and the breadth of the land; a Government under which our beloved country would advance rapidly in the highway of prosperity, honor, happiness, and glory.

JANUARY 6, 1888.